The D.A.D. Factor

3 Keys That Unlocked My Life

Glen E. Gibbs

Mindset Mastery: Book 1

The D.A.D. Factor © Copyright 2022 Glen E. Gibbs

All rights reserved. No part of this publication may be reproduced, distributed or transmitted in any form or by any means, including photocopying, recording, or other electronic or mechanical methods, without the prior written permission of the publisher, except in the case of brief quotations embodied in critical reviews and certain other noncommercial uses permitted by copyright law.

Although the author and publisher have made every effort to ensure that the information in this book was correct at press time, the author and publisher do not assume and hereby disclaim any liability to any party for any loss, damage, or disruption caused by errors or omissions, whether such errors or omissions result from negligence, accident, or any other cause.

Adherence to all applicable laws and regulations, including international, federal, state and local governing professional licensing, business practices, advertising, and all other aspects of doing business in the US, Canada or any other jurisdiction is the sole responsibility of the reader and consumer.

Neither the author nor the publisher assumes any responsibility or liability whatsoever on behalf of the consumer or reader of this material. Any perceived slight of any individual or organization is purely unintentional.

The resources in this book are provided for informational purposes only and should not be used to replace the specialized training and professional judgment of a health care or mental health care professional.

Neither the author nor the publisher can be held responsible for the use of the information provided within this book. Please always consult a trained professional before making any decision regarding treatment of yourself or others.

For more information, email glenegibbs@gmail.com.

ISBN: 979-8-9861896-0-4 (Paperback)

Any references to historical events, real people, or real places are used fictitiously unless otherwise stated. Names, characters, and places are products of the author's imagination.

Front cover image by Gibbs Innovative LLC.
Book design by Gibbs Innovative LLC.

Printed by Gibbs Innovative LLC, in the United States of America.

Second printing edition 2022.

Dedication

I would like to dedicate this book to everyone who made a meaningful contribution to my health and well-being. If I have ever smiled at you then you know who you are.

Table of Contents

Introduction		5
Chapter 1	The D.A.D. Factor	11
Chapter 2	Mindset	17
Chapter 3	What Shapes You	25
Chapter 4	Narcissists	31
Chapter 5	Unlock Your Intentions	37
Chapter 6	Unlock Your Mood & Attitude	47
Chapter 7	Unlock Your Disposition	53
Chapter 8	Unlock Your Inclinations	59
Chapter 9	Learn	67
Chapter 10	Leverage	77
Chapter 11	Choices	83
Chapter 12	Next...Desire Higher	91

Introduction

"Transformation isn't sweet and bright. It's a dark and murky, painful pushing. An unraveling of the untruths you've carried in your body. A practice in facing your own created demons. A complete uprooting, before becoming." Victoria Erickson

Success

"Success always makes sense."
Mindset Master Key #172

If you ever wondered why some people seem to be satisfied with the same, more, or less than you are, it is because their desires are different. One person who desires to survive will be satisfied with something different from someone who desires to surpass. What they focus on and where they put their energy will be different. One person may desire to supersede a relationship, and another may desire to survive some sickness. Even if you find someone who has the same desire to succeed in the same way that you do, that desire may lie in another area of their life. Everyone's definition of success differs from yours, which is why success is always personal. In every case, success fulfills one of the five following desires:

> Success can mean fulfilling a desire to surpass.
> Success can mean fulfilling a desire to supersede.
> Success can mean fulfilling a desire to sustain.
> Success can mean fulfilling a desire to subsist.
> Success can mean fulfilling a desire to survive.

Transformation occurs when a person's current definition of success is no longer acceptable. Surviving is no longer acceptable and is replaced with the desire to subsist. Subsisting is no longer acceptable and is replaced with the desire to sustain. The next transformation comes when sustaining is insufficient, and you want to supersede, become "the next." When you are ready to "shock the world," you desire to surpass and accept nothing less than being the absolute best.

What is your broad definition of success? Granted, success is relative and varies depending upon what aspect of your life is being looked at, but I am asking about your big picture definition. Is your definition of success fulfilling a desire to survive? Do you simply desire to escape adversity? Is your definition of success fulfilling a desire to sustain? Are you satisfied with being a little better than who or what is around you? Are you content with simply making it from day to day? Is your definition of success fulfilling a desire to supersede and be "the next" whatever? Do you desire to surpass and become "the one and only"?

Origins

I have been an ordained Deacon, a licensed Minister, and an ordained Minister; same collar, different leash. I spent over a decade doing a deep dive into what I call "Contemporary Western Theology," more commonly known in the USA as Christianity. I thought my effort in this area was a milestone that marked my "arrival," but it was just a stepping stone to where I am today.

I have never cared whether or not others believed what I believe; I still don't. If the theory had a basis, then it warranted further pursuit. I came to my own conclusions, which were not popular because I was always the boy who told the emperor he was naked.

I spent years studying books that were not part of the mainstream to find consistent answers. I put in work because I never took things at face value, which may also be the source of my conflict with organizations formed based on collective thought.

"Tradition eliminates the need for leadership."
Mindset Master Key #81

While in the midst of religion, I read a story, and it hit me differently. At this time in life, my focus was on distinguishing between problems and symptoms. I would look at symptoms as problems and vice versa to see multiple sides. I had always viewed the following story as a problem; a "that dude was jacked up" perspective.

When I reread Luke 8:26-39 KJV, a story about Jesus and the man from Gadara, I looked at his situation as a symptom, not a problem. I had an epiphany.

*26 And they arrived at the country of the Gadarenes, which is over against Galilee.
27 And when he went forth to land, there met him out of the city a certain man, which had devils long time, and ware no clothes, neither abode in any house, but in the tombs.*

I wondered how he got that way. I know what it was like to intimidate others unintentionally and be confined for reasons beyond your comprehension, so I felt a kinship with that man. The revelation I received was that his father dropped the ball. I was not sure what that meant at the time, so I spent many years after this revelation analyzing what I discovered and testing the merits of my observation.

35 Then they went out to see what was done; and came to Jesus, and found the man, out of whom the devils were departed, sitting at the feet of Jesus, clothed, and in his right mind: and they were afraid.

In investigating my theory, a series of profound spiritual encounters resulted in my being divested of my demons, just like the man in the story.

**"People's people problems are either
problems with people with problems problems
or problems with people's problems problems."
Mindset Master Key #17**

Confinement is not always physical; prejudice is a form of confinement. If you have ever heard "you are just like..." or "you got that from..." you have been pre-judged. If you have been pre-judged, you have been confined in some way. Another form of confinement comes from being improperly prepared to lead a productive life. In this case confinement comes in the form of unforeseen limitations.

The level of pre-judgment and improper preparation in my life led to my becoming overwhelmed by my issues instead of uplifted by my abilities. These issues contributed to how I was confined because the people who should have been freeing me to be myself were putting me in chains that constrained my growth. It was a circular thing where my problems were created by the same people putting me in chains. In their eyes, I was all I would ever be. I was never free to deal with my demons.

38 Now the man out of whom the devils were departed besought him that he might be with him: but Jesus sent him away, saying,
39 Return to thine own house, and shew how great things God hath done unto thee. And he went his way, and published throughout the whole city how great things Jesus had done unto him.

Once I understood the nature of my chains, I unlocked my life. After my life was unlocked, I completed this book.

**"Nobody will value you more than you value yourself."
Mindset Master Key #160**

Become Aware of Your System of Existence

Your "**System of Existence**" is a term I created to describe my personal ecosystem. It encompasses the sum of everything in my environment, how I perceived everything in my environment, combined with how I interact with everything in your environment. The D.A.D. Factor provided a perspective that helped me uncover clues about the "location" of my best System of Existence.

The mindset summarizes your System of Existence to produce your moods and attitudes. Your mindset encapsulates your inclinations and disposition within your values and externalizes summaries of your System of Existence as intentions. Your mindset development is proportional to the level of improvement to your System of Existence. Making significant mindset changes requires substantial changes in your System of Existence.

Your D.A.D. Factor affects your mindset, and your mindset affects your success. When migrating to another System of Existence, be aware that your D.A.D. Factor plays a significant role in the System of Existence you select. If your D.A.D. Factor is lacking the results of your efforts will fall short of your expectations because your selection will be based on an incomplete perspective of the System of Existence you are migrating to.

"Everything isn't for everybody."
Mindset Master Key #11

Get In Where You Fit In

"Fitting in" is what happens when two Systems of Existence are compatible. Effective assimilation happens when there is a high level of overlap between your System of Existence and that of others. Ineffective assimilation is when one unsuccessfully attempts to overwrite one System of Existence with another one. Finding your tribe or clique are examples of effective assimilation. Culture shock or being "a fish out of water", racism and bigotry are examples of ineffective assimilation.

Keep in mind the need to balance the dissimilarities between your System of Existence or social ecosystem and that of others if you want to make significant advances towards your goals. The people who have already arrived at your goal may or may not have a compatible System of Existence, so do not assume they do based on your common destination. Even when you have reached your destination you still may have not arrived.

There is never a simple solution to a complicated challenge. Many factors contribute to the types of interactions people have with one another. The individual cannot control every one of them, which complicates things. However, the individual can take control of their contribution to the interaction. There are always goals that one can achieve by taking the correct steps to navigate the landscape of their existence. I had little control over what happened to me, but I did control my contribution to my situation and the path to my goals.

Lock & Key

The Lock: Locks

Locks limit access to what is valuable. Some of what people are looking for is not missing or lost; it is simply locked up. What they need are the keys.

Safety and security are priceless, and whoever desires control the most seeks the keys. Your desire to control your life must be greater than anyone else's. If you do not have your keys, you need to get them; it is up to you to unlock your life.

My environment created my locks. It was utterly devoid of usable direction, advice, and defense. Unfacilitated expectations were the norm, so my level of responsibility and accountability were disproportionate to the resources provided. Doubt, fear, anger, shame, terror, failure, frustration, and hopelessness were the ingredients in my bowl, a recipe for going crazy.

The Key: Seek Your Keys

Transparency is a key. It is not easy to always share what is on my mind. I believe that being transparent about my past is worth sacrificing my privacy. My intention is to help someone climb out of their situation.

My original intent was to create a list of life rules which I wrote down for my children to reference. These life rules are where my journey as an author began. The D.A.D. Factor is the first book that grew from this set of life lessons.

I really "desire" for you to understand that people do things for a reason, yourself included, whether they know the reason or not. If you want to change your life, change what you do. To change what you do, you must change your reason for doing it. If you are going to change your reasons for doing what you do, you need to understand why you do it in the first place.

Chapter 1 The D.A.D. Factor

"No matter what you're going through, there's a light at the end of the tunnel and it may seem hard to get to it but you can do it and just keep working towards it and you'll find the positive side of things." Demi Lovato

The D.A.D. Factor

Direct "control the operations of; manage or govern."
Advise "offer suggestions about the best course of action..."
Defend "resist an attack made ... protect from harm or danger."

Factor "a circumstance, fact, or influence that contributes to a result or outcome."
languages.oup.com/google-dictionary-en/

At a minimum, a person's mindset should be competent in directing, advising, and defending that person. When caregivers do a good job, people grow up to lead a balanced and productive life. When caregivers fail, the people may have lifelong challenges, some of them debilitating. In this book, direct, advise, and defend, a.k.a. "The D.A.D. Factor," are the keys to unlocking your life and eliminating limitations both known and unknown.

The D.A.D. Factor is the sum of the effects of everything that contributes to how you manage your life, navigate your challenges, and protect yourself from harm or danger. The acronym D.A.D. is not gender-specific; it measures the quality of your experiences with the authority figures in your life, primarily your caregivers. The main focus of this book is on two things: how you got where you are, and second, what to do to change the trajectory of your life.

We are born with the expectation to be directed, advised, and defended, and we expect these three things to come from your caregivers. We also expect these same caregivers to teach us how to direct, advise, and defend ourselves. Caregivers orchestrate circumstances and exert influences that contribute significantly to who you are and how you see the world.

I noticed that successful people had at least one person in their life who made the sacrifices that allowed them to consistently present the best version of themselves. Successful people also have people in their lives who are willing to be a resource, people that can be relied on in times of difficulty, which instills a level of confidence.

Ultimately, you have to build your own confidence, be your own resource, and rely on yourself in times of difficulty. If you have someone to guide you in this process, you are ahead of the game. If no one has filled this role, you have to make the sacrifices to make sure you consistently present the best version of yourself.

You never live that same day more than once, but you may do certain things the same way every day. Do you do certain things the same way every day and feel like you are not making any real progress? What will you do about it? You know you need change, but what needs to change? How do you know if you are changing what needs to be changed and not changing what needs to stay the same?

The point of "The D.A.D. Factor" is not to identify flaws; it is to give you the ability to consistently see the connections between what you expect, what you experience, and how you respond. When you see these connections, make strategic changes and not changes based on trial and error, as I did.

To assess your D.A.D. Factor, examine the nature of the challenges you face; the patterns that emerge will point in the direction you need to look to find solutions. "The D.A.D. Factor" focuses on the processes associated with finding out what your mindset is doing now and what your mindset should be doing by uncovering what influences, affects, and impacts your mindset.

"The D.A.D. Factor" enables you to self-teach, providing an "environment" that strengthens your trust in your intuition. You will have a lot more "aha" moments. As you interact with what is around you, two things will happen; first, you will experience an increased perception, and second, you will become better able to recognize opportunities; increased perspective.

Like driving a car, the D.A.D. Factor is like identifying what need to moving forward in life. A person's D.A.D. Factor determines how rough the road to success is or, in other words, how effective and efficient your efforts are when it comes to reaching your goals. When one's "D.A.D. Factor" is low, the road is bumpy and full of twists and turns; when it is high, the road is smooth and straight.

Do you have goals? Do you set goals? Do you achieve your goals fairly regularly? Were you adequately equipped, prepared, and enlightened in a way that allows you to achieve your goals without undue hardship? If the answer is no, "The D.A.D. Factor" is not adequately present in your mindset. If the answer is yes, then "The D.A.D. Factor" in your mindset is relatively high. If your D.A.D. Factor is low; start by setting small goals and as you achieve them, set more significant goals. If your D.A.D. Factor is high, then use what is in this book to help someone else.

I had to become my own D.A.D., a director, advisor, and defender of myself, out of necessity. Assuming this role proved helpful in the classroom, business, and personal life. The skills I acquired in the process were instrumental in my development. The principles and practices I developed proved to transfer seamlessly across most of my interactions. I have had success as a parent, a teacher, a volunteer, a business owner, author, innovator, speaker, coach, and consultant by utilizing what I discovered.

Determining Your D.A.D. Factor

The process of identifying your D.A.D. Factor in its current state establishes the starting point on your journey to becoming the best possible version of yourself. Clearly understanding where you are equips you to look forward and backward objectively.

Direct means to manage or govern.
> How much structure was in your life?
> Was the structure balanced across every part of your life?
> Were some things structured and other things random?

Advise means to offer suggestions about the best course of action.
> How much advice and guidance were present in your life?
> Was the advice productive or counterproductive?
> Do you feel confident about outcomes based on this advice?

Defend means to protect from harm or danger.
> What was your level of personal safety and security?
> Do you believe you have help if you make a mistake?
> Do you believe that you only have help if you make a particular type of mistake?

You had Direction, and Advice, and Defense if:
> Your life was well-directed, well-advised, and well-defended
> You had a closely-knit and functional family
> You had sufficient provisions and care
> You had great advice and guidance
> You lived within a safe, secure environment
> Your environment provided you the opportunity to grow
> Your environment enriched your body, soul, and spirit

What Is Your D.A.D. Factor?

To determine your D.A.D. Factor identify which of the eight combinations best apply to your life. While deciding whether or not you had direction, advice, and defense, keep the process as simple as possible and take the "yes or no" approach.

An Overview of the different D.A.D. Factor Combinations					
	Direct	Advise	Defend	Yours?	Rank
1	YES	YES	YES		BEST
2	YES	YES	NO		
3	YES	NO	YES		
4	YES	NO	NO		
5	NO	YES	YES		
6	NO	YES	NO		
7	NO	NO	YES		
8	NO	NO	NO		WORST

Based on this list, everybody has a one out of eight chance of being jacked up in some area of their life and need to evaluate their mindset balance in some way and fix what is missing. What is most important is determining if any D.A.D. Factors are missing, not why. The blame game is a waste of energy and does nothing to change your caregiver's lack of ability.

Challenge yourself to reevaluate what you consider normal. Not questioning your motivations leads you to accept a low D.A.D. Factor as "normal." The mindset will subconsciously gravitate towards familiar people, places, and things without asking why you are drawn to them. Always question "normal". Focus on what needs to be fixed.

Lock & Key

The Lock: Your D.A.D. Factor

The lock is one of eight possibilities. Some combination of direction, advice, or defense existed in your life. The lock is the combination of which ones were present and which ones were missing.

The Key: Take Charge

To unlock your life, you must desire to take charge of your direction, advice, and defense. You cannot totally rely on others for this. I learned all too well that few people have a deep desire to provide direction, advice, and defense for others, and the few who do sometimes do not do it very well.

How much productive direction did you receive?
On a scale of one to ten, how self-directed are you?
Who gave you direction when you needed it?
Who was primarily responsible for providing your with direction?

How much productive advice did you receive?
On a scale of one to ten, how self-advised are you?
Who gave you advice when you needed it?
Do you trust your judgment?

How safe and secure did you feel growing up?
On a scale of one to ten, how much do you have to self-defend?
Who defended you when you needed it?
Do you have trust issues with authority figures?

Do you need to change the way you make decisions?
What needs to stay the same in your decision-making process?
What needs to change in your decision-making process?

What goals have you set and met?
What goals have you set and failed to meet?

How does your caregiver's efforts affect your decision-making?

Chapter 2 Mindset

"I want to give all the knowledge I can give; that's what I'm here on earth to do." Timbaland

Interactions

To "unlock your life" is to evaluate your interactions and put them into one of four categories.
The interactions that add to the positive parts of your life.
The interactions that add to the negative parts of your life.
The interactions that take away from the positive parts of your life.
The interactions that take away from the negative parts of your life.

Constructive people cultivate productive interactions that take away from the negative and add to the positive. Destructive people cultivate counterproductive sources that add to the negative and take away from the positive. The objective is to cultivate productive interactions.

What does the word "mindset" actually mean?

By definition, the mindset includes your: Moods, Inclinations, Intentions, Attitude, and Disposition. *www.Dictionary.com*

These words' commonality is that they are the result of processing information presented by a particular environment. Your mindset acts as the bridge between your conscious mind, your subconscious mind, and the rest of your world. The gateway between you and the world around you is the mindset, and you are the gatekeeper.

The mindset is like a material made up of elements with a non-specific orientation. When this material comes in contact with a polarizing force, the material becomes less random and more oriented towards the polarizing force. With iron, this process is called magnetization. In the mindset, this relates to the Law of Attraction.
https://www.successconsciousness.com/blog/law-of-attraction/law-of-attraction-definitions/

The critical point is that YOU control the contact with polarizing forces. You also control the amount of polarization you experience and can actually "self-polarize." Another way of looking at this book is that it helps you understand how you are polarized, how the polarization happened, what polarization you need to achieve your goals, and finally, how to change the polarization to what it needs to be.

The combination of information coming from your senses of sight, hearing, taste, touch, and smell constantly update your mindset, continually influencing your adjustments to your Moods, Inclinations, Intentions, Attitude, and Disposition. Your mindset decodes the information based on how your mindset is encoded or, in other words, how you process the information you get from your environment. The way your mindset is encoded is impacted heavily by your upbringing, nurture, or lack thereof. This is why two people can simultaneously engage in the same thing and have entirely different responses to the experience.

Your environment dictates the quality, quantity, and diversity of information your mindset has available. Your environment forms the foundation of your mindset. Your expectations are influenced by what you experience the most. When you change your setting, you change your experiences. When you change your experiences, you change your expectations. When you change your expectations, you change your results.

My First Prototype

My earliest memories revolve around traveling to Mississippi from Nebraska for our summer vacation. I distinctly remember the metallic smell of sun-heated fabric, getting car sick, and the swimming pool at a motel in Springfield, Missouri, the favored stopping point on a journey into the unsettling strangeness of Mississippi.

I had a toy truck, it was one of those red plastic toys, durable but inexpensive. Pretty much just a piece of plastic for the body and wheels that did not turn. I was around four years old. I remember that this was when I made cornflakes with milk and flour instead of sugar; I couldn't read yet. I ate it all even though it tasted terrible. I have always believed that it was my responsibility to get out my situations.

This truck was pretty dull; it just rolled, and I had to go and get it and roll it again. I got my sisters to play with me, but eventually, my sisters got bored. I still do not know how I came up with this idea, but I found a couple of rubber bands in the hotel room, tied them to the front axle then attached them to the rear axle so that when I pushed the truck away from me, the rubber band tightened, and the truck would roll back. I remember that I thought that was pretty cool.

I have always been highly innovative and creative. The solution or path just pops into my head. It does not matter what is involved; I creatively manipulate it if it moves. Things like metal, wood, software, words, relationships, thoughts, dancing, music, and food are all things that move, and I come up with innovative and creative ways to "rearrange" them.

Until recently, I never knew why I was this creative. I came across articles and books that relate creativity to trauma. Trauma is a counterproductive surprise with long term effects. I think creativity comes from "not trusting true" and a desire to find a path back to normal. I believe that the subconscious can direct the mindset to manipulate its existence proactively; creativity.

The Three T's

What frames your mindset are the three T's, what you have been *Taught*, how you have been *Trained*, and what you have been *Told*.

What you are **Taught** affects what you believe.
How you are **Trained** affects what you do.
What you are **Told** affects what you think about or imagine.

To change the framework of your mindset, you have to **reteach, retrain** and **retell** yourself. You can reshape your mindset in whatever way you choose. The first challenge is to discover your current framework. Next, determine what your framework should be. The third part is changing your framework to what it should be.

Make sure your mindset is based on internal desires and not external influences. Your mindset is just like anything else with structure, changing something critical on a whim can cause a collapse. Likewise, adding to a structure without a plan can create obstacles or barriers. Adding and taking away from your mindset both change its framework and can affect your ability to utilize your mindset fully. Actions without intention yield unintended results.

You must reteach yourself if you want to change what you believe. What makes this challenging is you have to unlearn what you have learned. Trust in yourself is the main issue. If you believed something and found later it was not true, what makes you confident that your judgment is good enough the second time around to put you on the right path? When you reteach yourself, use verifiable facts.

Do not "fill in the blanks," meaning that if there are twenty questions you need answers to before you believe something, answer all twenty and do not let any of the questions slide. 9 out of 10 is not good enough. Incomplete information and assumptions are one of the reasons mistakes are made, and reteaching is required in the first place, believe me when I say I know this firsthand.

To change what you do, you must retrain yourself. Put structure in place then recondition yourself to embrace habits and patterns of behavior that are productive within that structure. Discipline comes from structure, but all the structure in the world will not result in retraining if you are not determined to change your behavior and are not persistent within the scope of that structure.

When you retrain yourself, use small, closely spaced stepping stones. Make small permanent changes instead of large temporary ones. Success builds confidence, and confidence is critical for lasting change.

"Everybody has the right to be wrong."
Mindset Master Key #79

To change what you think or imagine, you must rewrite the narrative playing inside your head by retelling yourself. The challenge is telling yourself the truth. Remember when I mentioned "not trusting true"? Something is true if it works for you, and something is the truth if it works for everyone or everything or everywhere.

I caution you against accepting the consensus as truth because if the foundations of the consensus are flawed, then everything built on that consensus is flawed. Accepting consensus as the truth is one thing that puts me at odds with various institutions, primarily theological. Their remarks about how "thousands of members surely cannot be wrong" and my reply that "I was pretty sure there was enough room in hell for a few thousand" didn't help.

"Make it earn it" is one of my mantras. Nothing I use in the process of retelling myself gets the benefit of the doubt. If it is the truth, meaning it always works the same way, every time, everywhere, for everybody, I use it; otherwise, I leave it where I found it.

To reteach, retrain, and retell yourself, you must have determination. Anything less than absolute success must be unacceptable. The results of your efforts will expose the flaws in what you have been taught, how you have been trained, and what you have been told. Do not let emotions like shame and disappointment drive your changes when you find these flaws. Use those feelings to fuel your determination to succeed.

When I say determination, I mean it in the sense that you will not veer off course because of obstacles, options, or opportunities, real or imagined. If you are dazzled by the glitter, you run the risk of not seeing things for what they really are. When you lack focus, you become vulnerable to confusion. Keep your focus on your goal. Do not give up, do not give out, do not give in!

Nurture

Nurture is like a mold used to form your mindset. There are two fundamental molds. The first is Organic or Intrinsic Nurture, meaning belonging naturally; essential. The second is Inorganic or Extrinsic Nurture, which means coming or operating from outside.

Organic Nurture allows the mindset to grow and develop with support and care. There was a willingness to do what it takes to identify what the molded mindset needs to grow and develop into what it should be. Organic nurture is about caring and nourishing. One characteristic of organic nurture is shaping and grooming based on a goal-oriented delayed gratification model. Another is actively seeking an optimal environment for development and vigorously defending individualism.

Inorganic Nurture focuses on reshaping. The inorganically nurtured mindset develops within the confines of the caregivers' preconceptions. Inorganic nurture is slash and burn. Any part of the mindset that does not fit the caregiver's preconceptions is cut off, seared, and burned to prevent further growth. Short-term thinking, following blindly, busy work, and immediate gratification is indicative of an inorganically nurtured mindset.

Your mindset was molded by your caregivers. They designed and "made the mold" based on their mindset. Their mold was based on how someone else molded them. What kind of shape are you in? Did their mold help your personal growth and resiliency? Were you molded with limiting beliefs, limiting language, behavior, or actions? Did your caregivers do a good job, or do you need work?

Keep in mind that how your caregivers created the mold for your mindset may not have been entirely up to them. There are instances of people doing what was done to them. They never bothered to question why they did it or why they believed it was right. In other cases, caregivers choose to go against the grain and break the mold instead of doing what has always been done for reasons long forgotten.

Just because children have similarities to their parents does not mean they are copies. What worked in the past will not seamlessly translate to the next generation. My point is that if, when it came to shaping their mindset, none of your caregivers chose to "break the mold," your mindset might be a hand-me-down.

Go Fish

My dad taught me that fish only bite when it is raining, which he thought was true. I discovered later that it was not. I did not like standing in the rain waiting for fish to bite, so I only went fishing with him once at Carter Lake in Omaha, Nebraska. I remember standing on a brick wall watching him fish. We had on raincoats. He caught a catfish and a couple of "bass-looking" fish. We never ate them. He buried them in the yard beside the garage. Weird that I remember that so clearly.

A single mother raised my father in the 1930s. Growing up on a farm in the deep south during the Great Depression meant that he probably only had time to do what he wanted to do when it was raining. I guess he never bothered to question the connection between what he believed and why he believed it. Do fish only bite when it is raining, or do I only catch fish because the only time I go fishing is when it is raining?

In contrast to this, my uncle took me fishing on a sunny day, and we caught more fish that one time than I had ever seen my dad catch in my whole life. Their efforts differed because of what they were taught, how they were trained, and what they were told. These two men had been taught, trained, and told different things, so their thoughts about what was true were different.

Lock & Key

The Lock: The three T's

The lock is the mold used to create your mindset. The mold shaped what you have been taught, how you have been trained, and what you have been told. In every area of your life, some form of guidance existed, both productive and counterproductive.

The Key: Get Detailed Information

To unlock your life, you must individually address each aspect of your mindset. Start the process by revisiting what you have been taught, how you have been trained, and what you have been told.

Your mood, attitude, intentions, inclinations, and disposition need individual attention. Look at what you do based on what you believe. Look at what you do without question, then ask yourself why. Examine your mold and break it if necessary.

What were you taught that you still use to this day?
What were you taught that you later had to reteach yourself?
What have you had to teach yourself?

What training did you receive that you still use to this day?
What training did you receive that required you to retrain yourself?
What training did you do yourself?

What were you told that you still believe is true to this day?
What were you told that you later found to be untrue?
What major conclusions were your required discover on your own?

Was your nurture organic or inorganic?

Chapter 3 What Shapes You

"For everybody in the world, the answers to the mysteries in your life usually lie in your childhood, your upbringing, and your parents." Kevin Macdonald

**"What shapes you is the combination of what you are up against and what you get hit with."
Mindset Master Key #159**

Eight Forms of Forgiveness

My secret weapon is forgiveness. Forgiveness takes work. My first instinct is to go to war, but a fist is not resilient. Not embracing the actions of others makes it easier to let things go.

You can choose to try and justify the transgressions of others by internalizing their actions and risk living a life filled with anger and bitterness. You can also choose to swallow the painful pill of forgiveness, genuinely heal, and move on.

Ultimately your most challenging task is to forgive, which unleashes more productivity and growth than anything else you can do. No one can take away your power to forgive.

Eight Forms of Forgiveness are:
Forgive other people for what they did to you.
Forgive other people for what was done to them.
Forgive other people for what they did to others.
Forgive other people for what they missed regarding you.
Forgive other people for what they missed regarding themselves.
Forgive other people for their contribution to your challenges.
Forgive yourself for what you did not do.
Forgive yourself for what you did.

Forgiveness is like giving your mindset a clean place to rewrite who you choose to be. Unforgiveness to the mindset is like writing on notebook paper with spray paint, nothing can be rewritten.

"Forgiveness has no flavor." Mindset Master Key #33

**"Just because you got beat doesn't mean you got beat."
Mindset Master Key #183**

Counterproductive Direction

My sisters and I would sit in the backyard and repurpose materials salvaged from a house my dad tore down. Our job as kids was pulling nails out of flooring and hammering them straight to use them again. We made a game out of everything, so we still had some fun even though we did not play the same way the other kids played.

I was in a room designated as the library. My father asked me to gauge the position of one piece of salvaged wood he wanted to nail to another piece of wood. He was downstairs asking, by yelling, whether or not the board was in the proper position. I said yes, then no, and then I said I was not sure. In my defense, I wasn't sure what the actual goal was. I distinctly remember the board; it was Hunter Green. I am sure that if I went back to that house and knocked a hole in the wall and looked, it would still be there.

He said, "I am going to hammer the board into place and that if it wasn't right," then...some garbled response... which translated into nothing good for me. He hammered the board in, came up the stairs to where I was, took one look, and came utterly unglued. All I remember is being jammed face-first into the bed and him repeatedly screaming, "You gotta make up your mind! You gotta make a decision!" while hitting me with a belt. This went on for some time. At some point where I stopped feeling pain, and all I felt was pressure.

This event is an extreme example of a lack of direction, a common theme throughout my formative years. One positive from this experience is that I can think abstractly very easily. I also create solutions to problems quickly. Another positive is that I do not second guess myself much.

The lasting effect of this experience is that I became "hyper-decisive". It is pretty much the end of the matter once I make up my mind. I try to look at every available "side" of a situation beforehand to compensate for this. Another challenge is that I rarely ask anyone for anything personal, and if I do, it is seldom more than twice.

"People do what makes sense to them."
Mindset Master Key #20

Counterproductive Advice

My father owned a house on Spencer Street. The tenants had dogs that they kept in the basement, and they made a mess. I learned firsthand that maggot-infested dog shit has a distinctly repulsive aroma. It was the summer between second and third grade if I remember correctly. This house was about a quarter-mile straight up the street from my house. As always, I was the kid who was the gopher for my dad. I remember making multiple trips back and forth to get things from home and bring them to him. On the last trip, I carried some cleaner from a lady neighbor who said I should add one capful to 5 gallons of water or something along those lines.

I walked downstairs, and the stench was so foul I just dumped the whole jar, maybe a quarter cup, into the bucket. I just wanted to get out of there. One would expect a chemist, which he was, to adjust to the solution; that did not happen. Here is what did happen. He made a weird noise, grabbed one of those old school irons with the cloth cords on it, ripped the cord off the iron (wow), and yelled, *"What did she say?"* every time he hit me with it.

Keep in mind that since that day, I have had concussions, broken bones, torn muscles, dislocated fingers, stitches, stage two hypothermia, and second-degree burns, but nothing comes close to the pure, raw, fiery pain. If this has happened to you, I do not need to describe it, and if it has not happened to you, you will never understand.

The story is indicative of an extreme example of a lack of advice. There are not many positives to this experience other than discovering I have a deep sense of empathy. The disparity between my expectations in this case and what I experienced left a deep lingering scar in my mindset.

I became a highly literal person due to this experience, meaning that I do not understand subtext, hints, or innuendos; allusions go straight over my head. I have not figured out how to fix this yet.

"Lies convey a lack of respect."
Mindset Master Key #67

Counterproductive Defense

My father gave my sister a ride to a swim meet at her middle school. I decided to tag along. The plan was to drop her off at her swim meet, and then we would go to Westroads Mall. The mall is around seven miles from my house on 4029 Miami Street in Omaha, Nebraska; I googled it. I do not remember the date, but I know it was snowy and cold, nothing new in the Midwest. We dropped my sister off and went to the mall. I was excited because of all of the G.I. Joe toys they had. I knew I would not get one, but I was satisfied with looking at them.

We arrived at the mall, and I distinctly remember asking permission to go an aisle or two away from where my father was looking at pants to play with the toys. I knew beyond a doubt that if I wandered away from where I said I would be, I would have to walk home. He said, "Ok." I got caught up playing with the toys and lost track of time.

I had not moved from the spot I started at, so I figured everything was ok. Imagine my shock when, while enjoying myself, I felt that something was off. I went to where he was, and sure enough, he was gone. I looked around the store, and yup, he was gone. I guess a normal kid would have been afraid or scared and would have gone to an authority figure for help. Not me; I got mad.

I took off and started walking home. One productive thing we were all taught was how to find our way home. I learned to navigate the city before I was in kindergarten. It was snowing very hard when I got outside, so visibility was low. I had a pretty good idea of getting home, so I headed that way. I found out later that I was walking home in one of the worst snowstorms ever.

I guess I had angrily stomped about a mile or two down the road when he pulled up beside me. He had left me and went to pick up my sister. She opened the car door and started yelling at me to get in. But I was so pissed off I told her no and kept walking. He was laughing his ass off; he thought it was funny.

I got even angrier and kept walking. She turned and started screaming at him in a way unique to teenage girls, then reached out and grabbed my snowsuit and yanked me into the car. I tried to jump back out, but she wasn't having any of it, so I ended up staying in the car and riding home. He lied, period.

"Never get bit by the same dog twice."
Mindset Master Key #3

The effect of this incident is that I could care less about what a person *says* they are going to do. I look at what they do and what they have done. In fact, the more you use words to try and convince me the less likely I am to believe you. Additionally, I developed a healthy skepticism of people, especially ones in authority.

The Shift

These three incidents are a few of the many that highlight why it was necessary to become my own D.A.D. Factor. I had to facilitate my transformation from what I was to what I needed to be. I eventually stopped looking at things as good or bad, holy or evil, right or wrong. I transitioned to looking at things in terms of productive and counterproductive. The result of this shift was that I gained a lot of insight into why people do what they do. I also learned to try and avoid getting caught up in what they are doing. The benefit was a greater sense of peace, more balance in my entire life, and more success.

Lock & Key

The Lock: Mistakes

The counterproductive actions, inactions and interactions create locks. Focusing on failures keeps you bound. Expecting others to hold themselves accountable for their actions blocks the locks from opening.

The Key: Redo

To unlock your life, understand the experiences that shaped you, then reshape the parts that need it. Nobody knows with 100% certainty how their actions affect you, and some people would not care even if they knew. Your redo is on you; it is your responsibility to redirect, readvise, and "redefend" yourself based on what you see in yourself, even if nobody else does.

What past experiences shaped you the most with regards to you directing yourself?

What past experiences shaped you the most regarding how well you trust your judgment?

What past experiences shaped the way you perceive your safety and security?

What is your most productive personality trait?
Was it developed from a positive or a negative experience?

What is your least productive personality trait?
Was it developed based on a positive or a negative experience?

What limitations do you experience that seem like a glass ceiling?

What are your best & worst experiences based on your own actions?

What are your best & worst experiences based on other's actions?

Chapter 4 Narcissists

"You should never view your challenges as a disadvantage. Instead, it's important for you to understand that your experience facing and overcoming adversity is actually one of your biggest advantages." - Michelle Obama.

The Nature of The Narcissistic

You never know where you may encounter a narcissist; it might be on a date, at the altar, at work, in the pulpit, at school, or at home. Regardless of how they got into your life, you still need to know how to deal with them. Their preferred prey is a warm and engaging person who seeks to make a meaningful contribution to the lives of others.

I have coached, counseled, and mentored many people who were either in narcissistic relationships or were suffering the aftereffects. These are people who are hardworking, respectful, and generous. As I have spent more time coaching high-performance individuals and keynote speaking, I am amazed at how many people find themselves in a relationship with a narcissist. No one is immune, present company included.

I can only speak from personal experience about how it affected my mindset. I know without a doubt that if you do not know how to direct, advise, and defend yourself properly, you become vulnerable to exploitative personality types. The way you are exploited is directly related to deficiencies in your self-direction, self-advising, and self-defense. Sometimes the exploitation is direct and other times it is subtle. The key to identifying a narcissist is how they interact with YOU. Even though other people think they are saints, to you they are anything but that.

Narcissists seem to gravitate towards people who get satisfaction from helping others. Even after the relationship ends, many victims try to reconcile their expectations of reciprocity, still trying to make sense of that past situation. Others start to question their sense of judgment and often overcompensate in future relationships, distrusting people and never allowing the new person to earn their trust.

"Never share what you care about with people who do not care about you."
Mindset Master Key #7

A narcissist will make you seem like you are essential to what they want to do; you aren't. They are just trying to figure out what to say and do to get what they want from you. They tune into your buttons and what it takes to push them. You have to be very observant and objective to keep from getting sucked in. It is not as easy as it sounds.

Their real goal is to be able to deny you your desires. If you are open and candid about your desires, they will make you believe their promises and not honor them. Sometimes they take a disruptive stance just for the sake of being disruptive because your frustration pleases them.

When a person grows up being nurtured by a narcissist, they will have challenges in life that an average person does not. When a narcissist nurtures you, you are on your own financially, physically, soulically, and spiritually. If you need any direction, advice, or defense, you must supply it yourself. My one saving grace was that I knew that my "normal" was not normal from an early age which led me to be skeptical of everything.

Whenever I had a question, it was always marginalized, belittled, or made into a joke. I as regularly referred to as a "moronic ass son of a bitch." Most of what I asked about was "mumbo jumbo bullshit." I was literally and frequently told that my questions were "moronic." The exact phrase was, "I ain't got no time for moronic ass questions." So, around the age of eight, I stopped asking any heartfelt questions. I learned to internalize my desires, starting somewhere around ten or eleven; I became an expert at repression.

Your self-confidence is what suffers the most damage from a narcissist. A narcissist hates independent people and will do anything to destroy your sense of self. They love sabotaging your efforts and take great pleasure in their ability to cause you discomfort. Psychological pain is their favorite, but physical pain is an acceptable substitute if that doesn't work.

A narcissist will ALWAYS be an abusive, neglectful, undermining, and sabotaging person (A.N.U.S.) by nature. Once again, some are direct and others are subtle. They are great actors. The potentially confusing part is that they will put on all of the appearances that they are a caring person, often in a publicly embarrassing way, like if you experience an injury that requires a doctor and they did not cause it. You may think they care, they don't.

Their public and private personas are very different. So different that someone who has only experienced their public persona has difficulty believing their private persona is as bad as it is. They use this as a form of self-defense, deliberately directing attention away from how their neglectful nature may have contributed to your condition. Publicly they are seen as hard-charging go-getters, intelligent, type A, generous, understanding, and passionate. Privately they are something different altogether.

Control

A narcissist wants to be in absolute control of your wants, needs, and desires. They get an immense sense of satisfaction from telling you "NO" or what they will not do. Their ability to dictate your disposition makes them happy. It does not matter whether telling you "NO" makes you happy or sad. All they care about is that their words have power over you.

A narcissist will also use money to manipulate your emotions. One trick is that they come off as a person who has money, then get you to base your self-worth monetarily, finally denying you access to their money and thus damaging your sense of self-worth. They combine this with manipulating you into undervaluing yourself and, voila, an instant inferiority complex.

A narcissist will always give you $4.99 when you need $5.00. They will always "come up short" at the last minute. They find disappointment delicious. Any attempt to open a discussion ends in "anger," which is just an act; inwardly they are happy. They want your emotions to run wild. They love to bait you out of your safe place with a promise, then go back on their word just to watch you struggle. I learned to earn what I get and get what I earn.

**"Asking more than twice is begging; never beg."
Mindset Master Key #200**

You learn from a narcissist to never, ever ask more than twice. Asking more than twice is begging. Asking them for anything is another thing that makes them feel powerful. I very rarely ask anyone for anything for myself for this very reason. I have gotten a little better as I have gotten older, but asking is still one of my toughest challenges. I prefer to do it for myself or do without it. On the infrequent occasions where I ask for myself, I very seldomly ask more than twice.

The Remedy

When you are a "nice" person, being indifferent is against your nature. Do it anyway. Cold neutrality works wonders. They want you to be a hard and apathetic person, so treat them that way. Trying to win them over is a waste of time. Keep your emotions in check; emotion fuels their enthusiasm. The way to neutralize a narcissist is indifference. Treat them like they do not matter, they don't.

A narcissist wants you to always be on edge, waiting for "the other shoe to drop." Confusion is what they use to put you in a state where you never know what will happen next, good, bad, or nothing. They will never stop trying to create discomfort. They will make you happy only to make you more unhappy later. They feed on emotion. They make promises knowing they will not keep them. They make rules for you to follow and want to punish you for breaking them, but they want forgiveness when they break their own rules. The best thing for you, and the worst thing for them, is for you to be independent of them. My ultimate solution for dealing with a narcissist is to get away from them and "don't need."

**"There is safety in distance."
Mindset Master Key #149**

Lock & Key

The Lock: The Narcissist

Interacting with a narcissist will tie you up in knots. Focusing on trying to make sense of their activities keeps the locks closed. Not escaping keeps you locked up.

The Key: Neutralize the Narcissist

To unlock your life, neutralize the narcissists. Remove their direct or indirect influences. Reestablish your mindset based upon who you are. Pull up all the plants that grew from the seeds of a narcissistic relationship and burn them. Even after the relationship ends, these plants will still bear the fruit they desire, which is influence. Destroy any possibility of reemergence.

Have you successfully executed any major and complicated plans?

Do you quickly succeed regularly and often? Why?

Do you regularly interact with someone who consistently frustrates you?

What initial thoughts do your failures all have in common?

Who tells you "I told you so" when you succeed?

Who tells you "I told you so" when you fail?

Where do you need to be more independent?

Where do you need to take control of yourself?

Whose "no" do you need to ignore?

**"Once you make it over the mountain,
f(insert letters) the mountain."
Mindset Master Key #201**

This page left intentionally blank.

"Accept love, demand respect."
Mindset Master Key #110

Chapter 5 Unlock Your Intentions

"As long as your intentions are solid and about growth and progression and being productive and not being idle, then you're doing good in my book." Frank Ocean

Intentions "a thing intended; an aim or plan" *google.com*

Patterns

I discovered that I would always succeed to a certain point and then hit a wall. I could not move forward regardless of what I tried. It was depressing, and I called the feeling "being a spectator to success" I was close enough to success to do everything but experience it. I could change the people in my life, the places I worked and played, or the things I used, purchased and surrounded myself with, but the results were the same.

I might succeed for a while, but eventually, the success would slow to a stop. In some combination, I would either fail with the same people, fail in the same places, or fail using the same things. I would subconsciously gravitate towards what was familiar, putting me back on the same track towards the same results.

My pivot centered around my definition of success. First, I became more critical of influences. Then my definition shifted from an extrinsic definition to an intrinsic one. I focused on what motivated me and not what motivated others. I became less motivated by what "I was without" more motivated by what "was within me."

The intentions component of my mindset has always been strong. I have never lacked a plan; I have always had plans within my plans. Other flaws undermined my success like my reason for making the plans in the first place. Another flaw was my basis for what a good decision looks like.

My intentions early on were emotion-based, so my aims or plans did not yield the intended results. I got what I asked for but not what I desired. Emotions will get you started and keep you going for a while, sometimes years, but you will burn out before crossing the finish line.

Emotions are good for influence but not for endurance. I had to upgrade my foundation for decision-making to improve my criteria and make more success-oriented decisions. I started defining success for myself and stopped allowing other people to define it for me.

Success is an experience, not a feeling. The feeling should come from the experience. Seeking the feeling without the experience kept me off the trajectory to success. When I got back on track, I began to experience more success and to succeed more often.

**"If you do not see the problem,
then you cannot see the solution."
Mindset Master Key #57**

Evaluating your intentions is how you set your expectations which leads to a deeper understanding of your motivations. Once you understand your motivations, you can identify how to unlock your intentions. Unlocking your intentions opens doors to success.

Successful people have a mental checklist that accounts for almost every aspect of their lives. People who have been "given a leg up" in life have simply had this mental checklist ingrained in them as a part of their upbringing. Everyone else had to develop their mental checklist by trial and error.

I regularly see people get overwhelmed when figuring out what to do next. Lists help. As you become more productive, the mental checklist you need to succeed becomes more complex. Start with the basics, become consistent and efficient in executing the basic steps, then the complicated steps will fall into place much more straightforwardly, keeping you from being overwhelmed.

"You can't give someone a hammer and not expect them to hit something with it."
Mindset Master Key #44

The Grid of Intentions

When interacting with people, at places, or with things, always evaluate the intentions of everyone, everywhere, and everything involved. In some cases, you have to ask people directly, yourself included, "What are your intentions?".

Intentions towards the people, places, or things can be:
- To add to or increase the positive.
- To take away from or decrease the positive.
- To add to or increase the negative.
- To take away from or decrease the negative.

Pick an intention, a plan, or goal, of yours that fits into each of the four categories.

Add To Positive	Take From Positive
Add To Negative	Take From Negative

Clear intentions make it easier to prioritize and see what resources are available and create a list of what resources are needed. It helps isolate the objective and subjective aspects of a challenge by highlighting which denominators are constant, variable, the starting point, and the goal. Answering these four questions solidifies your intentions. The objective is to fine-tune your aim or plan; in other words, your intentions.

The Matrix of Interaction

The Matrix of Interaction is one of the most effective tools I have developed. I use **The Matrix of Interaction** to process complex challenges. When presented with a challenge either by life or a client, I frame the challenge using this tool. I created a cube-shaped physical object to represent the matrix. I use this cube in coaching sessions to make it easier for the client to visualize the process in three dimensions.

The Matrix of Interaction operates on the principle that there are six common denominators of everyone's life: people, places, things, time, talent, and treasure. The objective denominators are a person, a place, or a thing, and the subjective denominators are time, talent, and treasure. These denominators are in objective subjective pairs, people - talent, places - time, things - treasure where the first word in the pair is objective and the second word in the pair is subjective.

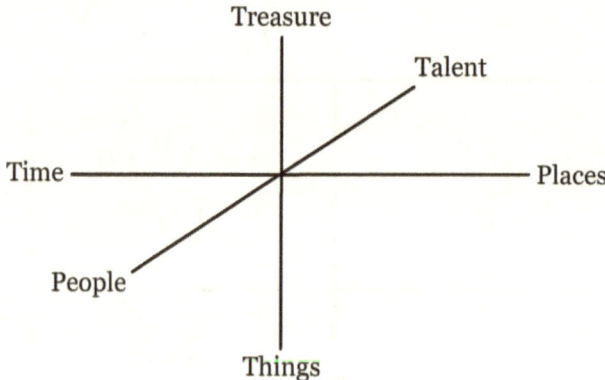

I created the pairings to isolate what something is from how you perceive it. The objective and subjective contrast between Things and Treasure, for example, is at the center of the well-used quote "One man's trash is another man's treasure" and is used to show that value is a matter of perception. The contrast between Talent and People isolates the fact that everyone does not always have the same views about talent. Time is purely perceptive and is most commonly used to establish a baseline for evaluating the energy required to eliminate the separation of Places.

Build Success If You Have To

You have both productive and counterproductive beliefs, thoughts, and actions. Put productive patterns of behavior and habits on autopilot. Gradually increase the energy spent in non-productive areas, making them increasingly productive, or eliminating them altogether.

Increase your effectiveness by making gradual increases in areas that need work. Resist the urge to focus all of your energy on areas where you are weak. Also resist the urge to put all your energy into areas where you are strong. Find balance, let solutions handle challenges, do not carry what you do not care about, stop embracing everything you encounter, and replace messes with processes.

A Matrix of Interaction Exercise

In this exercise my intention was to save Time. My starting point was Places meaning that Things were not where they were supposed to be: that left People, Talent, and Treasure available. The person, myself, used my systems and processes Talent to develop a plan, then I directed the use of my Treasure and acquired the lanyards.

Habit:
I always empty my pockets before sitting down when I get home.

Challenges:
I have bad short-term memory.
I hate looking for things and a terrible habit of misplacing keys.
I have an obsession with sets.

The System:
I use multiple brightly colored lanyards.
Each color represents an area of my life; work, home, and vehicles.

Result:
I can verify what keys I have by colors are and are not present.
Because of the bright colors it is easier to spot if my keys if fall out of my pocket while I am doing yard work.

The Gibbs Matrix

The D.A.D. Factor

		DIRECT	ADVISE	DEFEND
The Matrix of Interaction	TIME	Planner		
	TALENT			
	TREASURE		Financial Literacy	
	PEOPLE			
	PLACES			
	THINGS			Lock and Key

The Gibbs Matrix is an exercise that combines The Matrix of Interactions and the D.A.D. Factor. The goal is to identify whether or not you have what you need to sustain success. The objective is to clarify the direction, advice, and defense of the time, talent, treasure, people, places, and things that are a part of your plans. I have filled in a few spaces to demonstrate how this works.

To have a completely balanced life, you should have at least one entry in each space. Multiple entries in one space indicate that you have put more energy into that area than others. Strength comes from having an entry in every space; balance results from having a similar number of entries in every space.

Overcompensation is when you have multiple entries in some spaces and none in others which signifies that some aspect of your mindset needs unlocking. If you have five entries in the DEFEND - TREASURE space yet none in the DIRECT - TIME space, I would gather that there is a weakness in managing your time, and you have an obsession with the disposition of financial resources.

Keep in mind that creating this list of eighteen items is just the starting point. To sustain success, a plan, process, procedure, or structure needs to be in place to make sure each of the eighteen items on this checklist is capable of being maintained and leveraged for your personal growth and benefit.

Buy Success If Necessary

When I was a kid in Omaha, Nebraska, we had a store called Norton's As-Is, a type of thrift store. It was a dark, dingy, and funny-smelling place with all kinds of crazy stuff, including toys. It may not be accurate, but it was my perception that if I got something new, it would only be on my birthday or Christmas.

The challenge seemed to be learning to want what I got instead of getting what I wanted. I had the idea in my head that if I did not get it myself, then I would not get it at all; translation, I did a lot of scrounging and dumpster diving as a kid. Limited opportunities to "get" developed into a strong "make do" mindset.

My make-do perception, coupled with my compulsivity, creativity, and curiosity, led me down the path to becoming a notorious hoarder. If I thought that I might one day create something useful or cool, then I scooped it up.

Hoarding is not limited to things; you can hoard affection, attention, control, esteem, family, friends, freedom, relationships, success, influence, knowledge, talent, or even money. Hoarding is collecting large quantities of anything that has a perceived benefit. You might do something with what you have accumulated, but you "haven't yet" and probably never will. The feeling of "having" is more important than what is being collected. The perceived benefit is an illusion.

What you hoard will just pile up and require more time and energy to maintain. Shift your intentions from "make do" to "go do." Let go and free up your mental and physical space. Once you cross the emotional Rubicon, you become more productive, less stressed, and way happier!

To make the shift, I learned to be more excited about what is and less enthusiastic about what can be. The simple solution is to clearly distinguish what you "can do" from what you "will do." In my case, I simply adjusted my denominators upward enough to change my perception that Time and Places were more enjoyable than Things and Treasure. Now I take the less stressful option; if I need it, I don't make it, I buy it.

Borrow Success When You Can

Borrowing is how I made the most significant strides in life. I did not borrow objects or things; I borrowed strategies and techniques. Setting my intentions to focus on gaining through observation meant I got answers without asking questions and solutions before I had a challenge.

A simple story started when I was in college; my trial by fire. There was a group "meet and greet" for all the incoming freshmen that had food and lots of it. I did not recognize most of what was there. I can safely say that I was extremely ignorant, rough, and weird.

There were things I had never seen before, and I had no idea what to do. So, I went to the end of the line and let others go first. I stood there a while and watched what everybody else did, and then I did the same thing. When in doubt, be nice.

College was the first time I ever ate raw broccoli, cauliflower, and carrots, let alone dipping them in ranch dressing. I never knew that there were so many different types of cheese, and none of it had a red rind on it. I thought cauliflower looked a lot like pig brains, and broccoli looked like green pig brains. Nobody ate other stuff on the table, which is how I discovered what a garnish was; look but don't eat. College was where I also discovered that those really terrible doughnuts were something called "bagels".

Borrowing is one of the easiest ways to incorporate productive elements into your mindset. Borrowing is the best way to replace missing knowledge. Borrow techniques, borrow etiquette, borrow grooming, borrow strategies, borrow information, ideas and insights. Borrow anything your mindset is missing, try it on for size, and if it works, keep it.

What the Person lacked was Talent. I allocated Time which left Things, Places, and Treasure. Pun intended I spent Time learning through observation which enabled me to understand what to do with the Things in this particular Place which required no Treasure.

Lock & Key

The Lock: No Plan

Unrecognized patterns create locks. Counterproductive interactions strengthen the locks. The absence of a strategy blocks access to the locks.

The Key: Do Whatever It Takes

To unlock your life, take control of your intentions by examining your expectations of the people, places, and things in your life. If what you expect does not exist, it is up to you to bring it into existence by either building, buying, or borrowing what you need.

Take an active approach to how you direct, advise, and defend your time, talent, and what you treasure. Make sure that every method takes away from the negative or adds to the positive aspects of your life. Never repeat any experiences that add to the negative aspects of your life or take away from the positive ones.

Chapter 6 Unlock Your Mood & Attitude

"To increase our objectivity, we must learn to switch off the mini-movies. Objectivity requires us to be mindful, present in the moment, and experiencing what is happening without judgment."
Elizabeth Thornton

Mood "a temporary state of mind or feeling."
Attitude "a settled way of thinking or feeling about someone or something, typically one that is reflected in a person's behavior."
google.com

"People do not look for what they already have."
Mindset Master Key #222

If you had asked me, I did not have an attitude problem; I believed I was happy. I would later learn that this was not the case in the eyes of others. I did not realize people "were reflecting what I was projecting," which was my internal unhappiness and overinflated sense of self-importance. I believed I had already "made it" and did not need to prove anything to anyone. So yeah, I was arrogant. I needed to change, which happened after I unlocked my mood and attitude. And no, I was definitely NOT happy.

The Hard Way

I found myself struggling with challenges that were routine for other people. They had been equipped to meet their challenges and breezed past things that were significant obstacles to me. I was relegated to learning just about everything the hard way. My many shortcomings compounded my problems. I realized that I lacked direction, advice, and defense. My biggest challenge was ignorance, which slowed me down but did not stop me.

"Spend more time looking in the mirror and less time looking out the window."
Mindset Master Key #15

I wasted years trying to figure out what I needed to change about myself to become the type of person who was "worth the trouble." I believed that since I had the problem, I was the problem. I never was able to get it right; I was never quite good enough for other people. My breakthrough came when I started looking in the mirror to see how I was instead of looking out the window to see how everyone else was. I started working with what I had and built up from there.

I came up with the analogy that people climb, fall, or hold on. Climbers don't have the time to stop, fallers are trying to stop, and people holding on are just sitting there. It was not that others did not care; they could not care. People are focused on their situation and do not have the luxury of looking too long at what is happening around them. I first thought that I was plagued with unreliable, indifferent, self-oriented people until I realized that most people are just busy with their own lives.

Pivot

There was a pivotal incident in college where a fellow student explained that he had to get good grades to get into medical school because he had to pay his grandchildren's college tuition. He explained that his grandfather was paying his tuition and his great-grandfather paid for his father's tuition, which blew my mind; my whole attitude changed, the light came on, and my world shifted. I dedicated the rest of my days to disrupting the pattern and doing whatever it took when I had children. My mood went from "do this" to "be that."

At the center of the shift, my perception changed from seeing my future children as simply my offspring to seeing my children as my grandchildren's parents. My primary responsibility was developing my children into people who would be amazing parents. I changed the focus of my existence from wanting to become the real-life Tony Stark to doing whatever it took to make damn sure their childhood was nothing like mine. All I knew at this time was that where I was and where I wanted to be were different. My desire to find a way to remake myself, from patsy to patriarch, started the self-reinvention journey.

I read my great-grandfather's slave narrative on the Mississippi archives website, dictated before he died. From this, I was able to get some insight into the mindset of one of my eight great-grandparents. Even as a successful businessman, my great grandfather was not in any position to pay for my father, his grandson, to go to college, understandable given America's state in the early 1900s. I also knew my father could not pay for my children's education because he could not pay for mine. It was my responsibility to rewrite the narrative, literally.

One thing that contributes to my success is that I always have a primary objective. I ignore the noise and focus on my primary objective until I achieve it. Having a primary objective on top of a dogged determination made filtering out what not to do a lot easier. I keep putting one foot in front of the other, doing whatever it takes, no matter what.

"If the people around you had your answers, you would too."
Mindset Master Key #210

Plan A

My parenting strategy was simple, and it worked. I decided to do the exact opposite of what I experienced. I did a complete 180 of my upbringing. I also did not try to teach my children everything I knew; instead, I ensured they learned everything they wanted to know. The promise I made to them is this: they may not always get "the" best, but they will always get "my" best.

If they express an interest in anything, we drop everything to research the activity. I never said no without putting in the work. With five busy children, that ended up being a lot of work—thousands of hours at hundreds of different events doing whatever it took. When they surpassed my abilities to teach them, I paid somebody to pick up where I left off. This strategy boils down to directing, advising, and defending, even though it did not start that way.

At home, there was always music, laughter, weird noises from something I was building that would send them running either towards or away from me. The occasional hairspray flamethrowers were not uncommon. There were jokes, learning, teaching, swimming, music lessons, dance lessons, camping, cooking, shopping, water parties with epic backyard water slides, gardening. Endless accidents, hugs, and kisses, the words "I love you," calling out the wrong name in my loud "dad voice," mistakes, messes, and many life lessons.

I gave many answers to the many questions. We engaged in good eating, bad table manners, and memorable road trips. There were letters from teachers asking me not to help with Math. There was massive "bear-jacking" in Chattanooga. It's like carjacking only with kids and stuffed animals: countless games, unconditional support, birthday parties, smiles, encouragement, affirmation, movies, and many more byproducts of commitment.

I do not consider myself as extraordinary, I just see myself as simply doing my best to do what I said I was going to do. In the end, all I can say is that my kids always do the best they can with what they have. My Plan A seems to be working out.

Plan B

My "Plan B" is to share what I have learned with the world. I used my life experiences as content in this book to show what is possible. My superpower is that I always look for the best outcome. I believe everyone has a gift, a purpose, and value. No one is disposable.

Ultimately, I discovered that I had a few things in my favor; one was an insatiable curiosity, two was unwavering determination, and three was that I was good at delivering innovative solutions. One innovation is the adaptation of troubleshooting, a process I learned when trying to get to the root of a technical issue, to everything.

Troubleshooting can apply to anyone, anything, and anywhere. In its simplest form, troubleshooting requires that you answer three questions. What is "it" supposed to do? What is "it" doing now? What influences, affects, controls, or impacts the differences between what you expect "it" to do and what you "it" is doing now?

You can troubleshoot yourself by comparing what you desire to do with your life and what you are currently doing. Then examine what influences, controls, or impacts the difference between what you desire to do and what you are presently doing. If you are doing what you desire with your life, you should read this book with the intent of helping others. If you are not doing what you desire with your life, use what is in the book to help yourself.

"When things look more like what you envision and less like what you avoid, then you are headed in the right direction."
Mindset Master Key #120

Lock & Key

The Lock: Mood & Attitude

Your attitude affects your latitude. By this, I mean your attitude can limit your options which can create locks. When things do not go according to plan, exceptions to your expectations occur, your lousy attitude strengthens your locks. Lack of resiliency or, in other words, not taking a long hard look at yourself blocks access to your locks.

The Key: Direction

To unlock your life, you need to take control of your mood and attitude by looking at the experiences that contributed to them. Stay positive regardless of how the landscape looks.

Actively create new experiences that make productive contributions to your mood and attitude. Having a single point of focus simplifies decision-making. Be open to change if you find another plan more fulfilling. Grow more to know more.

Your attitude opens doors. Be a model prisoner if you are locked up and hope for early release from what is holding you back. Keep a positive attitude, even in a negative situation. Set your primary objective and focus on achieving that objective, use it as your driving force and stay focused on your one true desire.

When in doubt, be nice.

Chapter 7 Unlock Your Disposition

"Consult not your fears but your hopes and your dreams. Think not about your frustrations, but about your unfulfilled potential. Concern yourself not with what you tried and failed in, but with what it is still possible for you to do." Pope John XXIII

Disposition "a person's inherent qualities of mind and character." *google.com*

The quality of anything is directly related to what it is composed of, and the mindset is no different. Your disposition is what reflects the quality of what is in your mindset. Garbage in garbage out, so you will have a trashy disposition if you fill your mindset with trashy information. When you are not intentional about your disposition, it is like walking around with an empty bucket and letting anyone put whatever they want in it. I guarantee that eventually, it will get filled with everything that has oozed, flaked or been scraped off of other people.

"You can't carry 5 gallons of water in a 1-gallon bucket." Mindset Master Key #155

Your bucket

Your bucket represents what you are capable of accomplishing. What is "in your bucket" are your abilities. Everybody's bucket is the same size, and everyone has the same 24 hours in a day to put their bucket into play. So why are some people more successful than others? Success is a measurement of how efficiently you manipulate what goes in and out of your bucket. Carrying around counterproductive content in your mindset reduces your capacity for success.

Your bucket is almost empty when you are born, only containing the basics. As you get older, your bucket gets fuller because more things enter your bucket. Some things stay for a long time, and others leave after a while, depending on how you prioritize them. Lastly, there are the things that never make it into your bucket. These combinations of contents can get complicated, and mastering the balancing act becomes the challenge.

What is in your bucket depends on your nature and nurture. I have met people who only needed to make minor changes to the contents of their bucket. Their caregivers properly nurtured them, so they live their life knowing what they have and what they need. I have also met people who, because of a dysfunctional upbringing, had so much counterproductive content in their bucket that they could barely function. They were overly attached to an overwhelming amount of useless content.

Successfully making the upgrades to your mindset depends upon the quality and quantity of direction, advice, and defense that are present during the process of adjusting what is in your bucket. You may need to make radical changes to your environment in order to remove yourself from counterproductive influences. Be willing to supply the direction, advice, and defense yourself if it is not available from other sources. In the final analysis you are your responsibility.

Space

More space will be available in your bucket if you have an extensive support system and many available resources. You have to carry less of what you need to succeed personally; others share the load. On the other hand, if your support system is nonexistent, you have to carry everything in your bucket that you need to succeed, making it necessary to work harder for what you get and possibly take longer. The challenge, in this case, is to figure out what the bare necessities are and leave everything else behind, which is what I had to do.

In my case, I had so many things in my mindset that ranged from inconvenient to just plain wrong that it was difficult to isolate and identify each misconception. It was like I had hardened cement filling my bucket. Ever heard someone referred to as being "set in their ways"? This description implies that they are inflexible when it comes to adjusting what is in their bucket. Guilty as charged.

In my mindset, I found that "true" encapsulated the "truth," so I took a sledgehammer and kept hitting my beliefs until nothing was left to break. My method was crude but effective, and it was also time-consuming, wasteful, and painful, so it was a good thing I had learned to become comfortable with discomfort.

My goal was to make sure what was in my mindset earned its right to be there, so even though I wrecked a lot of relationships, burned bridges, and destroyed resources in the process of radically changing my mindset, it was worth it. I recommend using a gentler approach to isolating your truths, but not at the expense of success.

To succeed, you must have the focus, the desire, and the intent to reexamine everything you have been taught, all of your training, and everything you have been told. Understand that things will be stirred up within you while you are dealing with what is in your bucket. For me it was extremely painful. It is like shaking a snow globe; things you thought were settled came to light. Some of them might be unpleasant. You need to be resilient to deal with the inevitable revelations.

"Never do anything without a reason."
Mindset Master Key #1

Six Decisions

I had the opportunity to interact with people from all across the success spectrum and even helped a few people when they were on their way to becoming multimillionaires. I noticed that successful people work hard to keep their bucket empty and unsuccessful people work hard to keep their bucket full. An empty bucket has space that allows you to take advantage of opportunities quickly, but having a full bucket means change takes more effort.

There are "Six Decisions" you make that impact your capacity for success:

You decide what is not allowed into your bucket.
You decide what needs to be taken out of your bucket.
You decide what stays in your bucket.
You decide what is missing from your bucket.
You decide what temporary changes to your bucket are needed.
You decide on the reason for making each of these decisions.

Evaluate your decisions and keep adjusting them until the results of your efforts match your expectations. When you can make the most out of every opportunity you are presented with; you have a good grip on the Six Decisions.

Moderate the amount of emotion you allow when making the Six Decisions. Do not get "too up" or "too down." Your emotions are fuel for change. Make sure you put the fuel "in" the car and not "on" the car. Stay focused on your goals to get through the process.

**"You will never climb higher than you are afraid to fall from."
Mindset Master Key #66**

Your Rope

There are limits to what you can engage in and not experience some form of adversity. This limit is the "length" of your rope. The combination of your knowledge, wisdom, and experience determines this limit. Your knowledge, wisdom, and experience are interwoven together in your mindset, kind of like a rope. "Adding length to your rope" is what happens when you gain knowledge, wisdom, or experience.

When knowledge, wisdom, and experience increase, your ability to assist increases. The length of your rope determines the difference between experiences that have successful outcomes and experiences that end in adversity. Any new experience less than the length of your rope falls under the category of "been there done that." If the new experience ends in adversity, your rope is too short, and the experience is "chalked up as a lesson learned" when resolved.

Success and adversity both contribute to increasing knowledge, wisdom, and experience. The more adversity you overcome, the longer the length of your rope. The more you succeed, the longer the length of your rope. The depth of your experiences determines the strength of your rope. This visualization can also help you understand when you are overextending yourself or underestimating yourself. If your rope breaks, meaning you fail, your depth of experience is not enough. If your rope does not "reach" others, meaning your efforts "fall short", then the amount of experience you have is insufficient.

**"Frustration comes from expectation without facilitation."
Mindset Master Key #118**

Lock & Key

The Lock: Effort

Making poor decisions creates locks. The locks get strengthened when you simply hold on to behavior patterns instead of changing. Overextending or underestimating yourself keeps you locked up.

The Key: Your Bucket and Rope

To unlock your life, you must maximize your character's content. Treat your mindset like a bucket because it is critical to the quality of what you carry around with you. Use your bucket dynamically by regularly evaluating it using the "Six Decisions." Be resilient. Never do anything without a reason.

Balance your efforts to make sure all three components of your rope are the same length. Be conscious of overextending yourself beyond the range of your knowledge, wisdom, and experience. Be mindful of underestimating yourself and running the risk of missing out on opportunities or exercising options.

Chapter 8   *Unlock Your Inclinations*

"People usually think according to their inclinations, speak according to their learning and ingrained opinions, but generally act according to custom." Francis Bacon

Inclination "a person's natural tendency or urge to act or feel in a particular way" *google.com*

A Misadventure in Math

Multiplication tables have never made sense to me. Suffice it to say that I am not "good" at math. I have learned to do it, but it does not come naturally, and the old-school memorization strategy did not work well for me. The new way they teach multiplication, using pictures, is more like how my mind works.

I was in the third grade and I got a C in math. My father asked me what the problem was? At the time, I did not know. An eight-year-old third-grade child cannot produce a satisfactory adult answer, especially when interrogated in a menacing environment. All they see is someone screaming at them.

I was stressed, so I said the first thing that came to my mind, which was that I did not have a pencil. I immediately discovered that there is a bright light when you hit the back of your head really hard.

Streaks or specks of light in your vision are described as flashes. They can happen when you bang your head or get hit in the eye. They can also appear in your vision because your retina is being pulled by the gel in your eyeball. www.Healthline.com

I did not physically feel the effects of being punched in the face, but I got my bell rung pretty good. That is old school for a concussion. The rest of this particular discussion did not get any better.

From that point forward, I knew that finding the solution to my problems was my problem; expecting help was hazardous. My inclinations changed radically, and in addition to not understanding math, I learned to dislike it. Oddly enough, I was also in the third grade when I decided to become an Engineer.

Fast forward to sixth grade and fractions. Long story short, I got an F on my report card. I knew I was getting an F, so I took a blue pen and a black pen and whiteout to school. On the way home, I changed that F to a B. In my mind, if I got a right jab to the forehead for getting a C, then getting an F would be lethal. I still have this report card, and I have shown it to my children, and they got a good laugh out of it.

Fast forward again to my freshman year in college and a whole lot more math because studying to be an Electrical Engineer involves a lot of math. I struggled mightily. I was making plans to transfer to another school; I was at a loss when figuring out how to figure out what I needed to do. My nemesis was Calculus. My high school didn't offer Calculus; college was baptism by fire. I wasn't stupid; I still scored high enough on the standardized tests to get many college offers, including the Naval Academy and West Point; I was just ignorant.

One of the rare words of advice I have received was given to me by a senior. He simply said, "They would not let you in here if you couldn't do the work." Given that this was probably only the third or fourth piece of advice I had ever had that did not involve giving up, "do the work" is what I did.

I changed my inclination. I went from enjoying my freedom to focusing on staying free from living at home. I studied sixteen to twenty hours a day, seven days a week, had a nervous breakdown or three, then got up and commenced to continue to slam my head against the wall of ignorance. I managed to end the semester with an acceptable GPA. The biggest takeaway was that I developed a level of resiliency, determination, and confidence that still serves me to this day.

Not only did I stay at Vanderbilt, but I also graduated with an Electrical Engineering degree. My head bent, but the wall broke. I have learned and used around 16 different programming languages. I have worked as an Engineer, Design Consultant, Product Developer, Business Owner, Patent Consultant, and Instructor in Computer Engineering, Electronic Engineering, and Electrical Engineering. I even taught Calculus, my old nemesis. So just because you are not good at something does not mean you cannot get good. I was not good, and I got good.

Decisions On a Sick Day

When I was in fourth grade, the principal's office was green; oddly enough, I remember a lot vividly from this period in my life. Mr. Tarantino had a thing for African Violets. They hung everywhere in the office. I had a decent reputation with the administration because I was a quiet kid. Hard to believe if you know me now.

On this day, when I went to the office and told them I was sick, they believed me probably because I was ill for real. I was dizzy, and things were blurry. I discovered later that I had the flu. I asked if I could call my mom to come to pick me up. They let me use the phone. I called the phone number that told the "time and temperature" then proceeded to have an imaginary conversation with the recorded voice.

The people in the office did not know that I was faking it, so when I told them I needed to meet my mom at the entrance to the school, they were ok with it. She didn't drive, but they didn't know that. So, I left the building, walked to the end of the school driveway, and sat there. After a while, the adult who watched me eventually tired of waiting and went back into the school; this was my cue.

I quickly ran across the street and down the hill towards home, a few miles away. I made it as far as the park then I started getting dizzy and vomited. I was miserable; in addition to being sick, it was cold and rainy in a misty, depressing way. I needed to lay down, so I crawled under an evergreen tree, made a bed of needles, and went to sleep. I woke up later, feeling a little better. I got up and kept walking until I got to where my mom worked and told her what I had done.

"You gravitate towards what is familiar."
Mindset Master Key #117

She was pretty upset that I did not call her. I was nine years old, and the only time I ever remember getting a ride home was on the city bus in Omaha, which was for one year of my life. I probably got picked up from school, but not often enough to remember. In Omaha I walked home if I forgot to ask for bus fare. So, expecting someone to come to pick me up because I asked them was out of the question.

I am not saying that I never had a ride home the years I attended school. In my mind, anything about me was "on me," the cavalry always seemed to be busy. Nobody ever checked with me to make sure I had what I needed to do what I wanted, so why would today be different? I was very sick and needed to leave, so I could not leave it up to chance. Yes, I lied, but according to WebMD, children lie to establish behavioral boundaries and my boundaries were broad.
https://www.webmd.com/parenting/guide/child-at-7-milestones#2

"Prepare yourself to react to survive, prepare yourself to act to succeed."
Mindset Master Key #146

Damaged Is Not Defective

**"Never let your past experiences limit your future ones."
Mindset Master Key #169**

The difference between **defect** and **damage** is that **defect** is a fault or malfunction while **damage** is injury or harm, the condition or measure of something not being intact.

https://wikidiff.com/defect/damage

"Damaged" and "defective" are two different things. Damage to your mindset does not automatically make it defective. However, being damaged by life can introduce imperfections into the mindset. The point is that when you repair the damage, it reduces the effects of the imperfections.

For example, if you measure the weight of a soda can then put a dent in it, the weight does not change because the can is the same materially. The measurable difference is that the dented can has less capacity. It still holds the soda, just less. When you try to refill it, you will find that the dented can will not hold as much as the undented one.

Like a dented can has a reduced capacity for contents, a damaged mindset has a reduced capacity for accomplishment. The evidence of "defects" in your mindset shows up in the form of not getting things to work out as they should or as a "stuck" point you cannot seem to get past no matter what you try.

When you cannot seem to affect outcomes, something is missing and some aspect of your mindset needs adjustment. Ask yourself, where do I get stuck? When do I get stuck? How or why is that place, time, or thing always a point where progress becomes a challenge? Your "stuck points" exist because either deliberately, accidentally, or negligently an experience damaged your mindset.

To find the defects, take a deeper look at the experiences that shaped your mindset. To get past the influences of those experiences and achieve your goals, identify the incidents, isolate the issues, then repair the damage.

I focused my efforts on increasing my capacity and knocked out a lot of dents in the process. I took the maximum advantage of every opportunity to challenge myself. These efforts changed my inclinations in a way that allowed me to leave home and stay gone.

My new environment was where I thrived. I was in the presence of limitless opportunities to self-improve, and I became a little less dented with each passing day.

Lock & Key

The Lock: Expectations

Counterproductive interactions create locks. Not knocking out the dents strengthens the locks. Ignoring the impact of counterproductive interactions blocks access to the locks.

The Key: Insight

To unlock your inclinations, examine why you act and react the way you do. Look back on the experiences that shape your responses to the people, places, and things in your life. Examine yourself. Identify any damage to your mindset, regardless of how it happened, and put together a plan to "knock out the dents."

This page left intentionally blank.

"Become your own expert."
Mindset Master Key #136

Chapter 9 Learn

"The keys to patience are acceptance and faith. Accept things as they are, and look realistically at the world around you. Have faith in yourself and in the direction you have chosen." Ralph Marston

**"Assistance should be a luxury, not a necessity."
Mindset Master Key #68**

Self "a person's essential being that distinguishes them from others, especially considered as the object of introspection or reflexive action." *Oxford Languages*

My inner voice challenges me to both "find my best where I am" and to "find where I am my best." By best, I am referring to two things. The first thing is to find your best relative to your expectations, your internal best. The second is to find your best relative to the expectations of your System of Existence, your external best. If your internal or external best is less than required, you need to put in more work. If either is more than required, you are not challenging yourself.

Finding your best, where you are, becomes easier when you adjust what is within your **System of Existence**. Making changes to what is around you reveals why you are not at your best in certain situations. Mix up every aspect of your life until you start experiencing yourself doing better. Start by spending the most time around what brings out your best. Next, start changing what you do and how you do it, then see if your best is still good enough for where you are.

Finding where you are your best is easier when you change to another System of Existence. Start by spending more time in places that bring out your best. Change places you go; try spending time outside areas that are normal for you. When you go to another location, work with different people, then examine whether or not the outcomes are acceptable. While in a new place, try doing the same thing you did successfully in your previous System of Existence.

Connect the dots, and then examine how certain combinations of people, places, and things contribute to your results. You will start to see what is available to fight with and what you need to focus on fighting. Notice--I did not say *who*, but *what*.

Getting into conflicts with people is a waste of time. Win or lose; you will subconsciously gravitate towards the same type of people and spend most of your life in some kind of conflict. The only person you can truly change is you. You have to learn to win from within using resources at your disposal to find your best where you are, and find where you are your best.

This process is like deactivating the tripwire on a booby trap. Focus on disarming the deficiency because once you change yourself, you will be amazed at how quickly the counterproductive people, places, and things simply disappear. BOOM!

"You always have four options:
   1. Shut Up and take it.
   2. Speak Up and say what you think about it.
   3. Get Up and walk away from it.
   4. Give Up and go along with it."
Mindset Master Key #5

Direct "control the operations of; manage or govern. aim (something) in a particular direction or at a particular person." *Oxford Languages*

Learn To Self-Direct

"If one advances confidently in the direction of his dreams, and endeavors to live the life which he has imagined, he will meet with a success unexpected in common hours." Henry David Thoreau

In this age of endless information, there isn't any excuse for not having a clue. Three things are critical to being self-directed, desire, intent, and focus. These three things combined will amplify your efforts in a way that they cannot separately. When intent, focus, and desire are combined they highlight what is important.

When I was in High School, I only received two pieces of advice that helped me determine how to reach my goals. Dozens of teachers, coaches, and counselors had the opportunity to help but never made a single meaningful contribution to my decisions that led to a lifetime of success. Some actually made it their business to discourage me.

Miss S wasn't even one of my teachers. She was simply a kind, soft-spoken southern lady who expressed a genuine love for all students, not just those who looked like her, which was rare. I received a letter from a University I liked, mainly because of their football helmets, and asked her about it. She said, "It is a good school if you can get in." Unlike other staff at the school who openly stated that I was too stupid to go there or I would flunk out if I went anywhere, she simply said it like it was. In the end I enrolled and I graduated.
Thanks, Miss S.

The second teacher told me that my grades would be better if I came to school more often. I worked more hours and I worked later into the evening than I was supposed to, so I was tired a lot. I could have stayed at home all the time, but I wanted to live a little. Spending my life trapped two right turns a mile north of the middle of nowhere was not an option. If I wanted school clothes, gas money, and to eat school lunch regularly, that was on me.

I am glad I had a job because I had to save two weeks' wages to pay for my college application. My father would not pay for it because he wanted me to go to the local school in-state, no help there. Classic narcissist moves. Realizing I needed balance, I cut back my hours and made it to school more often.

This same teacher encouraged me to compete academically in state and regional academic events. Because of her, I got exposure from being involved in academic competitions. I won a few state-level academic awards, all of which helped me get into college with enough scholarships to pay for it myself. Narcissist neutralized. "Don't need".

Keep It Moving

People who always stay around the same people do it because the information they have is useless to anyone else. What comes out of their mouth is a combination of ignorance, fear, superstition, ill-conceived preconceptions, and bullshit. They spend their days swapping stupid from one bucket to another, a spoonful at a time.

Look at other people who take their advice. How is life working out for them? Their only original though was probably that they would not have any original thoughts. My point is this; when it comes to advice, most people do not know what the hell they are talking about. Forge your own path. Seek new people.

The people you need will meet you on your way to where you are going. Point your nose and toes towards your goals and not look left or right until you achieve them. It does not take a lot of outside input to succeed, just a few high-quality directions given at the right time combined with desire, intent, and focus.

**"Never share what you care about with those who do not care about you!"
Mindset Master Key #7**

Advise "guidance or recommendations offered with regard to prudent future action." *Oxford Languages*

Learn To Self-Advise

"I think it's crucial to have a feedback loop, where you're constantly thinking about what you've done and how you could be doing it better. I think that's the single best piece of advice: constantly think about how you could be doing things better and questioning yourself." Elon Musk

Usually, you need to be advised when you are at some point of vulnerability. You will never be 100% independent, so you will never be completely invulnerable. The risk is that when you ask for assistance, you may get a hand, or you might get a fist, a supportive word, or ridicule. Minimize the possibilities for counterproductive responses by developing the ability to keep your own counsel.

To self-advise, I created a list of insights, options, and perspectives I call a **Mindset Master Key**. Every item in the list has at least one story behind it. This list of Mindset Master Keys grows as I grow; there are over 200 on the list right now.

I simplify my insights into a summary of wisdom, knowledge, or inspiration. I use a phrase that is easy to remember and to the point. The keys work by acting as a preset trigger to change my mindset direction, approaches to take, or whether or not I should be proactive, reactive, or inactive in a given situation. These master keys disrupt counterproductive patterns.

The truth is a river and like a river every drop of water does not make from the start of the river to the end. Wisdom is the cup dipped into the river of truth somewhere along its route. This is why you will hear different people say variations of the same thing. It is not about who they are, it is about what they tapped into.

My Mindset Master Keys may not all seem to be wholly original, nothing is. We are drinking the same water as the dinosaurs. I created my list based on what worked for me, not to create points of contention. If they sound like something you have heard before then you probably have.

Here are a few of my favorites:

"People do what makes sense to them."
Mindset Master Key #20

"Everybody wants to be part of something good."
Mindset Master Key #12

"Everything isn't for everybody."
Mindset Master Key #11

"You teach people how to treat you."
Mindset Master Key #187

Self-advise, create your own master keys, **WRITE DOWN** personal observations. These are the milestones for your journey, which may mean nothing to others but mean everything to you. Existence is cyclical, so when you develop guidelines for yourself, you will know what you need to do "on the next go-round."

"Compete with what you are getting beat with."
Mindset Master Key #25

Defend "resist an attack made on (someone or something); protect from harm or danger. Speak or write in favor of (an action or person); attempt to justify. *Oxford Languages*

Learn To Self-Defend

"The two most important things to do for self-defense are not to take a martial arts class or get a gun, but to think like the opposition and know where you're most at risk." Barry Eisler.

You defend against threats, but what is a threat? It is simply someone else's intention to take action counterproductive to yours. The threat can be directed at you or someone or something you care about. After I learned never to let everyone know everything I care about, I found self-defending easier.

I summarize acting in self-defense as: *"The process of gathering resources that increase your readiness and raise your awareness, then strategically utilizing them to minimize or eliminate the impact of potentially counterproductive interactions."*

The essence of defense is the neutralization of counterproductive intentions within the context of those intentions. I have learned a few things about people, and one of them is that most people will not willingly engage in activities that are the "harbingers of pain." I refer to pain in the classical sense, derived from the Latin word poena, which means "penalty". The goal is to make interference not worth it to them. *google.com*

Self-defense has become second nature for me. I have recently become more diplomatic about my methods, but I "stay willing to burn it all to the ground," which means I am not afraid to start over if that is what it takes. Why? I know I can get all back.

"Silence can never be misquoted."
Mindset Master Key #22

You can also self-defend by mastering "the non-response," which avoids adversity by not accommodating expectations. The first non-response is not to say or do anything. Anything you say will get you deeper into a useless dialogue, so do not say anything. Steer clear of unproductive conversations; you will never get that time back.

The second non-response is simply telling them, "You have not earned the right to that answer." Let them know if they have not earned the right to the level of transparency they expect. Do not give away your hard-won sense of self; make them earn what they get from you.

The third non-response is to ask them a question without answering theirs; this works for nosy people. I have found that people who ask you many personal questions do not have your best interest in mind in the long run. If someone is interested in a mutually beneficial exchange, they will answer your question and ask theirs again. A person won't answer your question if they are not interested in sharing. I have seen people either walk away or ask a different question when I do this.

The fourth non-response works on narcissistic people. They are narcissists, and any form of manipulation, even getting you to respond to a question, encourages them. What you do is give them an answer to a completely unrelated and unasked question. If someone asks you a question that makes you uncomfortable, just respond with something like, "parallel parking is hard for me too," and smile. Eventually, they will get the hint and leave you alone.

Underhand Grip

My father usually treated me like a soldier in the Korean War, expecting me to wake up at any time and be ready to go. However, this morning, the usual streams of profanity and invectives were conspicuously absent when he came to wake me up. I took the win and went on about my day. Later I found out the reason for the change in his demeanor.

I discovered that he had attempted to shake me awake on an earlier occasion and I mumbled, "give me a few minutes." As a teen it was physically painful to wake up early. He persisted, and I repeated the same statement. Keep in mind that I slept facedown at the time. Somehow, I managed a "no-look underhanded reach-back throat pinch." I grabbed his throat with my thumb and one finger. I repeated, "give me a few minutes." He tried to pry my fingers from around his windpipe, and even though he outweighed me by over a hundred pounds still could not break the claw formed by my two fingers.

The years of hard manual labor he orchestrated left thick calluses on my hands and gave me that iron grip which backfired on his plan to bully me physically. He shifted tactics, but that is another set of stories. My point is that if you do not take a stand consciously, your subconscious will. This story is never not funny.

Lock & Key

The Lock: Ignorance

Ignorance creates locks. Avoiding responsibility for your destiny strengthens locks. Misplaced energy blocks access to the lock.

The Key: Learn

Learn how to self-direct, self-advise, and self-defend to unlock your life. You do not have to do everything yourself; just make sure it gets done.

"If you do not know, learn."
Mindset Master Key #46

Do you seek direction mostly from yourself or others?

Do you seek advice mostly from yourself or others?

Do you seek defense mostly from yourself or others?

Do you "talk out" your challenges? How is that working for you?

How much responsibility must you take for your safety and security?

How much do you trust the people in your life?

How much do you trust the places you go and the things you use intended to ensure your safety and security?

Do you work on developing your trust in your subconscious?

Chapter 10   Leverage

"I have great respect for the past. If you don't know where you've come from, you don't know where you're going. I have respect for the past, but I'm a person of the moment. I'm here, and I do my best to be completely centered at the place I'm at, then I go forward to the next place." Maya Angelou

When it comes to achieving your goals, you need to change what you do and how you do it. You have a choice between what you adapt and what you adopt. Adopt what someone else is doing or adapt what they have done to your situation. Your choice is to either integrate what is new into what you do or replace what you do with something new. You will experience life-changing results either way.

"You have not because you have not."
Mindset Master Key #209

Leverage

The word *leverage* has a few different meanings. According to Merriam-Webster.com, one meaning is "to use for gain," and another meaning from Google is " use (something) to maximum advantage." This means you use your abilities and capabilities for gain and to their maximum advantage.

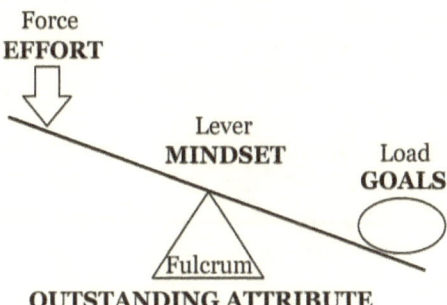

"What you can make happen is more valuable than what you can do."
Mindset Master Key #65

Your Lever

Attributes I acquired from my upbringing were not developed by choice, which meant I had to learn to embrace them. As a result of the adversity, I became creative, resilient, innovative, and afraid of very few things. Encouragement was non-existent, so my inner fire burns hot.

I felt like I was fighting a losing battle until I began to invest in self-improvement. I took advantage of growth opportunities as they presented themselves. The initial investment was supplied in the form of a few words of wisdom. To add to this, I read, attended retreats, workshops, and seminars.

The process of self-improvement can be direct or indirect. Self-improvement is a multifaceted activity so show gratitude for what you have, whether you got it directly or indirectly. In my case, many direct improvements came from indirect influences. A positive characteristic can result from a negative experience. Just because you may not like how something got into your "bucket" does not mean it does not belong there. What does not kill you makes you stronger.

I hated my father for a lot of my life. After he died, I began to see some benefits from my upbringing. What he did may or may not have been intentional, but there were some positive results from his methods. I got stronger physically, mentally, and spiritually. He was crazy AF, don't get me wrong, but amid the madness, there were some things that I "learned" that ended up being beneficial.

With all of the responsibility placed upon me, I grew up early. Very few of my desires were fulfilled by the efforts of others, so I became fiercely independent. I do what is necessary whether I want to or not. I make many more mistakes than average. I apologize a lot, but I keep it moving.

The education system in the deep south was just as brutal as my home life. People were cruel across the board, regardless of gender, race, creed, or color. I disagree that perception is reality. Brutality was my reality but I was not subsumed it; brutality was not my perception. So far so good.

Your Fulcrum

There is "that something" in your life that resonates through everything you are and do, that "go-to" gift you lean on whenever you face a challenge. This is your "Outstanding Attribute," the one thing you use regardless of what you are doing. Your Outstanding Attribute is what you use to maximize your leverage, the impact of your efforts.

Everybody has an "Outstanding Attribute"; they just have to find it. Start by looking at your approach to your challenges. Then fine-tune your search. There are free skills inventories, online tests, and many other ways to help you zero in on yours. Look at your life and find the common thread that connects your successes. What is it that you can successfully do with little effort?

If you are a visual problem solver, you will use a picture or diagram as your first option when encountering a new challenge. If you are a hands-on person, you will look at the structure of your challenges then try to take them apart to see how the pieces fit together.

Correctly positioning your Outstanding Attribute comes from finding your best where you are and finding where you are your best. Success is a process. Learn how to win using what is within you. You cannot wait for other people to produce an optimal opportunity for you; your success is your responsibility.

My message is that transformation is possible and does not need to take as long for you as it did for me. I learned to be more observant of what contributed to my success and began to see where I was getting in my own way. Some of my changes took years because of my stubbornness. Tune into the common thread that ties your experiences and personal growth together. This is where, why, and how you position your Outstanding Attribute which is what your success rests on.

"The worst rumors will be accepted easier than the greatest truths."
Mindset Master Key #127

Really Really?

After my first semester of college, I came home went to a local restaurant. At the greeter station was one of my old classmates. Mind you; I was in all the same Honor Societies and College Prep classes with this person every year of school. The conversation went something like this:

(Imagine you hear the background noise from a typical restaurant)
They asked, "How are you doing?"
I responded, "I'm fine."
They asked, "What are you doing?"
I responded, "Going to college?" (Demeanor change observed)
They asked, "Where?"
I replied, "Vanderbilt."
They said disrespectfully, "No; you are not."
I replied, "Yes, I am."
They said, "No, you are not."
I replied, "Yes, I am."
They said, "No, you are not."
I replied, "Yes, I am." (Denied thrice, lol.)
They said, "Let me see your ID."
(It is kind of irritating. I always seem to be required to have proof.)
I responded, "Here." as I handed it over.
(Needless to say, I was enjoying this exchange, not upset at all.)
They said, "Let me see your validation."
(If I remember, it was an orange card.)
I responded, "Here." as I handed it over.
They said, "Oh, **we all** thought you were in the military or prison."

I did not get a "great job" or "awesome" or "congrats" anything positive, mind you. I guess it was too much of a shock to their system. I never held their doubt against them. Yet another thing to laugh about. I understood my "Outstanding Attribute," properly positioned myself, and leveraged what I had to achieve my goals, much to the surprise of my classmate.

Lock & Key

The Lock: No Effort

Lack of intentional effort creates locks. Not investing in self-improvement strengthens locks. Improper positioning of your Outstanding Attribute keeps you locked up.

The Key: Put in Work

To unlock your life, do these things. First, invest in self-improvement. Put energy into actions that result in a personal net gain. Properly position and improve upon your Outstanding Attribute, the one thing you do best. Lastly, leverage every advantage you have at every opportunity to lift your loads and achieve your goals.

Your mindset is the lever and should be strong enough to support the weight of what you are seeking to accomplish.

You must dedicate yourself to producing the effort to lift the load, which are your goals.

Finally, you must focus on correctly positioning your Outstanding Attribute to maximize your success; this is your fulcrum.

What do you do to self-improve?

How effective are your efforts at self-improvement?

What is your Outstanding Attribute?

Do you leverage your Outstanding Attribute?

This page left intentionally blank.

"You fear what you do not understand."
Mindset Master Key #178

Chapter 11   Choices

"I would rather go to hell by choice than to stumble into heaven."
Benjamin E. Mays

Choice: Keep Moving Forward

I heard a story about a man who fell into a hole. Many people passed by and based their definition of helping the man on what they did for a living. A priest would say a prayer, a doctor would write a prescription, and a climber would throw a rope. One passerby jumped in, and the person in the hole said, "now we are both stuck!" the person who jumped in replied, "I have been here before; I know how to get out."

If someone is suddenly in the hole with you, make sure the person was not pushed in or did not fall in. If they are not there to help you, you are both stuck. I believe in jumping in then, seeing who you are, and assessing where you are as accurately as possible. My next step is to develop a plan, within your capabilities, to get you out of the hole. I am not worried about myself; I know how to get out.

Choice: Be the Sacrifice

Numbers 14:18 "The Lord is longsuffering, and of great mercy, forgiving iniquity and transgression, and by no means clearing the guilty, visiting the iniquity of the fathers upon the children unto the third and fourth generation." *kingjamesbibleonline.org*

At some point you have to decide to be the sacrifice, declaring to the universe that whatever happened before stops with you. You will catch hell, mostly from the living, when you declare yourself to be the fourth generation. You are in for a fight.

When something is sacrificed it is rendered useless relative to its intended purpose for the sake of something or someone else. In the case of breaking generational cycles, your lack of conformity to the consensus becomes a clear and present threat to the status quo which is always unwelcome.

Once you stir the waters there is no going back. When you decide to disrupt the flow of dysfunction, all that are swimming in it become acutely aware of their shortcomings. When you leave the chaos of generational confusion you will experience isolation and uncertainty. There is no script to follow so breaking the mold means you are almost completely on your own. When you "stay out" you "stand out" so I had to learn to get used to living life on the outer side of acceptance.

Choosing to "be" the sacrifice also means living a life centered around intent, desire, focus, and delayed gratification. I got tired of seeing generation after generation living with the aftereffects of the precursor to our current penal system. I recognized the game at an early age and chose not to participate.

Later in life I discovered principles that solidified my instincts, structured my determination, and put me on the path to success. It was not easy but it was worth it and in spite of largely being guided by faith. What I did worked.

Choice: Remember Your Victories

**"Everybody who is related to you is not your family, and everybody who is your family is not related to you."
Mindset Master Key #79**

Waking early in the morning before everyone and sitting on the corner of 41st and Miami Street in Omaha, Nebraska, was how I spent most of my summer mornings as a child. I remember the big Maple tree that caused the sidewalk to bulge upwards had created a perfect place to sit. Miami Street ran roughly East/West because I remember feeling the rising sun's warmth on my face as I looked towards 40th street and wondered what was beyond this scary, busy street at the bottom of the steep hill.

One day somebody built a go-kart. They rode it down Miami street, away from 40th, mind you, rolled right past the stop sign at the corner of 42nd street, and almost made it to the park on the corner of 43rd. We were all hooked.

Barry Green (not his real name) was my best friend in Omaha. Barry Green was a devil-may-care type of kid who always had a smile on his face and a heart for adventure. He was always a joyful participant in any of the neighborhood activities like kickball or hide and seek. We would build crazy forts in the backyard when it snowed and then have epic snowball fights.

When we were getting ready to race, every wagon, Big-Wheel, and lawnmower was in danger of being dismantled to supply parts for the competitions we had every weekend. We would roam for blocks looking for wheels, axles, and wood. We built and wrecked and rebuilt and raced over and over until it got dark.

I was one of the younger kids, so my skills and resources were limited, making my car slower and not as well built. On the other hand, Barry Green managed to find four Big-Wheel tires, and his go-kart was the envy of everyone.

The D.A.D. Factor / 86

Barry Green came over to my house to work on a new car, and he brought his enviable racing slick Big-Wheel tires with him. His latest design looked like the letter H with a seat. I can still see that go-kart to this day. It looked as fast as it was.

My go-kart was a long piece of wood without a seat. I attached the wheels from a wagon at the back and two small lawnmower wheels on the front. It had a narrow wheelbase, so it would tip over if I tried to steer it because it sat up so high. I would roll a few feet, and then BAM, I would face plant on the asphalt. I would hop up, flip it back over and keep going. That was my race, roll, then steer, then BAM, faceplant, all the way down the street.

It was race time, so we all lined up, and my older sister was my pusher. She still plays that role to this day, my pusher. She had my back before that was a "thing". The race started and like every other race, I went a few feet, and I hit the ground BAM. This time my sister was right there helping me and yelling "Go Glen" at the top of her lungs in that infectious way only a nine-year-old can. I was fully confident; I hopped back on and went another few feet, and BAM. Face, meet ground.

Undeterred, our race team persisted. I was rolling along pretty well when up ahead; there was a commotion. Everybody was running neck and neck right behind Barry Green. Then, suddenly, the letter H became the letter A, Barry Green began to spin in circles. He crashed into everyone, and they all wrecked except me.

I was rolling up to the pile-up, tried to steer around it, and BAM, face plant. My sister ran up to me and once again pushed me as hard as she could and said, "just go straight." I did. I crept past all the other go-karts and rolled down the hill in first place. I crossed the finish line, looked back, and then BAM.

I won that race with my sister and friend Barry Green's help. I like this story, not because I won, but because it taught me that fulfilling your desires requires a good push, a lot of encouragement, the ability to take advantage of opportunities that present themselves, and BAM, the occasional face plant.

Choice: Surpass the Negativity

"Dogs don't bark at what is inside their fence."
Mindset Master Key #207

Realize that words only have the power you give them. Taking control of negativity means that even though others have the right to tell you no, their "no" only has power when you give it power. You have the right to ignore them. Even if everyone you meet says no, that still does not mean that you have to accept it.

People will also perpetuate conversations about your past in an attempt to stay relevant to you. If they do not see the "new you", do not take this as a sign that you have not transformed; ignore the ignorance. Take this as an indication that they are unwilling to change and grow to know the new you. Smile, nod, and walk away. They are looking at the shadow of who you were and not the light of who you are.

Few people believed what I believed about myself. It seemed like people only repeated negative words. I pushed on past the noise, which is not as easy as it sounds. When you do right, doing right gets easier because you get better at it. Did the negativity affect me? Yes.

I overcompensated in most areas of my life which is a nice way of saying I developed a lot of compulsions and the associated challenges. My main challenge was that I made a lot of messes. I later learned that a mess comes from the absence of a process; actions with structure. I structured my actions and conquered my compulsions.

Figure out how negativity affects you and put energy into neutralizing its effect in your life. I discovered I had a strong subconscious tie between the words fear, no, failure, rejection, and punishment. Deep down in my subconscious, these words intertwined, tying my perceptions together in a way where these words meant the same thing.

I had to learn to dissociate fear, no, failure, rejection, and punishment from the word consequences in my conscious mind. Consequences is the word that formed the bond, so eliminating the connection of each word to consequences eliminated the limitations based on the word associations.

Realize that you cannot fix something with what broke it. If a person broke you that person cannot fix you. If a place broke you that place cannot fix you. If a thing broke you that thing cannot fix you. In my case it was a combination of the three so I had to leave the people, places, and things behind that were part of my "formative" years.

Negativity is the most widely used tool in relationships. It is easy to use because people have more experience with negativity than they do with encouragement. Do not use negativity as a tool. You cannot join wood together with the saw that cut it. The goal is for what is joined together to stay together.

If a parent was an alcoholic or abusive then becoming a narcissist or a drunk is not going fix the damage done to you. Learn to deal differently. Confronting the people that broke you won't work because all kids will play with a toy they broke. By this I mean they are going to do what they always did when they interact with you so nothing will change. Unless there is a spiritual component involved people do not change, they just act differently.

Choice: See Yourself as You Are

"Spend more time looking in the mirror and less time looking out the window."
Mindset Master Key #15

I have heard who I am not, what I am not, why I am not, and every other "not" you can imagine. I want to tell you this: if any input from others, especially negative input, does not lead to solutions, do not get frustrated. Some people are scraping the bottom of the barrel of intelligence. Find new people.

Everyone is not capable of getting you where you want to go. In my experience, only listening to what people say will not help you accomplish your goals. They will say whatever makes you feel good. Very few people have actionable information presented in an executable format. You will find that many people simply want to be right, relevant, or respected for their input.

Even when someone is sincere about your success, their roadmap starts with who they were before they made it, not who YOU are now. What this means is that until you get to the point where they started, what they did will not work for you. You have to make it from where you are to the point where they started before you can do what they did. Not being at THEIR starting point is why years of "help" from the gurus did nothing for me.

Your mindset is a combination of your moods, attitudes, inclinations, intentions, and disposition. You know that developing each part of your mindset requires a different approach. You understand how your mindset was formed, understand each aspect of your mindset, and how unlocking them is essential to your success.

How your starting point affects your success is why understanding your D.A.D. Factor is important. You need a way to take a "mindset selfie" to see WHO you are, AS you are, WHERE you are at any given instant. Your mindset is your responsibility.

Lock & Key

The Lock: Indecision

Not making choices creates locks. Lack of clarity strengthens locks. Avoiding painful outcomes blocks access to the locks.

The Key: Choose

To unlock your life, keep moving forward. Take control because you are the captain of your ship. Your word is law. Resist the urge to overcompensate for your shortcomings. Untie the "nots," counterproductive connections within mindset, before you try to detangle the truth. You have been there and done that; keep up the good work. Build on your successes.

"Done is when you are ready for next."
Mindset Master Key #180

"Ain't nothing to it but to do it." J.T. McGlowan

Chapter 12   Next…Desire Higher

"The key to growth is the introduction of higher dimensions of consciousness into our awareness." Lao Tzu

**"Everybody has the right to be wrong."
Mindset Master Key #79**

Working on myself is my life's work. What I learned to do, I learned out of necessity. What I do works, and hopefully, someone can benefit from what I learned. My motivation is that someone will be able to use what I shared to help themselves. At the end of the day this book is about what I did, you should follow your own path.

When making changes, the difference between molding and pushing is where the force is applied. When you apply force in one direction, things get pushed around. The result is that where you are is different, but what the force is being applied to hasn't changed. When you apply force in multiple directions, where you are is the same and what the force is being applied to is different. As you develop your approach to reshaping your destiny, try to challenge yourself in multiple areas of your life and you will change. Your goal is to mold yourself.

Reading some of the experiences I have described in this book was unsettling to some people. I had to relive them to recount them, so it wasn't a lot of fun for me either. If you find the stories unsettling, I want you to keep in mind three things:
1. You are fortunate not to have experienced them.
2. I used those stories to identify a point of impact.
3. I have many more stories about experiences that are worse.

My goal was to share what I have learned to provide options for others. The most challenging part of writing these books was finding the balance between usefulness, authenticity, transparency, and my desire not to seem like I am seeking sympathy; it is too late for that now, been there, "won that".

The Journey

Everyone started from somewhere, is somewhere right now, and is going somewhere. The word that comes to mind is trajectory. Intentions are set on every step of the journey. Some of the intentions are immediate, like getting a glass of water, and others are long-range, like graduating from college. When these intentions are set, influences are exerted on the mindset. These influences come from your past experiences, present environment, and future ideas.

Suppose someone does something, like making an unwelcome comment, for example, in an attempt to change your mood, attitude, inclinations, or disposition. In that case, they are trying to influence the trajectory of your life directly; what someone else does only has as much power over you as you allow. The question to ask yourself is how you could involuntarily enable them to have power.

There are known influences and unknown influences. You understand the results of known influences, whereas unknown ones create surprises because they result from unreconciled experiences. The significant departures from my optimal trajectory were the result of unknown influences. I did not realize what was getting me off track until I was too far in the wrong direction.

Just like a magnet can move a piece of metal, these influences can change the trajectory of your life by the way they interact with your intentions. To minimize the influences, you have to convert influences into information. Treat influences as opinions, not facts. When you do this, you create a conscious break that brings behaviors to the forefront of your conscious mind. When you are aware of your influences, you can control them.

Experiences can also instantly change your mood, attitude, inclinations, or disposition. Examine your memory and look for associations between past experiences and involuntary responses. Look for pivotal events as well. I have looked back, and discovered experiences that were powerful enough to leave a deep imprint on my subconscious. The question I had to ask myself is what provided that experience with its power.

Raising your awareness takes time, so do not get frustrated initially, do what you can and set your intention to do more. The benefit of this exercise is you will eventually find the truth. You may or may not like what you find. The goal is not to create a pleasant experience; the goal is to eliminate limitations. Physical scars can be seen and tied to the event that caused them; non-physical scars get covered by your behavior, and whether you see them or not, other people do.

After all the dust has settled at the end of the day, the journey is most important. This is what The D.A.D. Factor helps with the most, the journey. All efforts are for moving forward towards some goal. Gaining an understanding of your path to your goals comes from having the ability to actively provide yourself with direction, advice, and defense. Ask yourself often what you have learned and if you should do anything different to keep yourself headed in the right direction.

The Reward

I set my first life goal and achieved it. I set another life goal and completed that. I set a third life goal, which is in the bag as well. I spent a few years trying to determine my next life goal and achieved that one too. Now I am on my fifth life goal which it to help others from my newly discovered outlook on life.

Reaching each of my goals required me to become who I wasn't. In the process of becoming, I grew from who I was into who I needed to be. Each milestone along the trajectory of my success was marked by a significant transformation. A large part of each transition between the milestones was embracing who I had become. I do not always like who I become, but I am all I have, so I make the best of it.

Growth is not easy. Success requires a specific combination of elements in the right amount supplied at the correct time. If any one of these elements is missing, misplaced or misapplied then the entire process shuts down.

Each time I achieved a life goal, I better understood what combinations of elements produced the growth needed to reach that point. Each of the four life goals I achieved required different elements in different combinations. Interestingly enough, each life goal depended upon completing the previous one.

The process of rediscovering myself while in transition is what takes the most time, which plays a significant role in how long it takes to get to the next level. I began to document the patterns I saw during my transitions, which led to this book. In the end, the reward was the journey itself, the act of discovering how to produce the results, not always the results themselves.

**"If the nail goes in when I hit it with it then it is a hammer."
Mindset Master Key #220**

Love and Happiness

My latest transition involved looking internally at my mindset from a physiological standpoint. My efforts included correcting a sleep disorder that caused me to stop breathing every two minutes while sleep. I learned about nutritional deficiencies which were addressed. I increased my level of daily intentionality; I am more diligent about what I allow into my System of Existence.

My morning ritual was expanded to include declarations of daily intentions, motivational messages, guided meditation, affirmations and breathing exercises. I also added a cold shower routine which worked wonders for the lingering results of hypothermia.

The reward was that I rediscovered happiness. I realized that "not unhappy" was what my old mindset interpreted as happiness. Happiness is not just a function of the will, there are aspects of your brain chemistry involved as well. I can safely say that I am a completely different person than I was when I started writing this book six years ago.

I believe that, among other things, my dopamine levels were so low for so long that I forgot what happiness actually felt like. The most interesting side effect of this transition is that I see everything, everyone, and everywhere differently. Now I have to embrace this version of myself. I will self-direct, self-advise, and self-defend as I move forward into the newness of what comes next.

I Appreciate Your Time

I want to offer my sincerest thanks again as a small token of the deep appreciation I have for providing me with the opportunity to share. I appreciate the time you have taken from your life to read what I have presented here. Time is precious, and I am thankful for yours.

To my personal heroes I want to add that the support you gave me n m journey as an author speaks volumes to my heart and soul, both of which I poured into this book. Thank you, R. Davis, B. Deadrick, S. Horvath, T. Wilkinson (the tall one). They provided the push I needed when I needed it.

To everyone else I have ever met I want to thank you for being a part of the journey. I learn something from everyone I meet no matter how brief the encounter.

"It has been done; so, it can be done.
If it can be done, you can do it.
You can do it, so do it."
Glen E. Gibbs

Unlock Your Life!

References:

USGenWeb African-American Griot Project
http://msgw.org/slaves/gibbs-xslave.htm

Braverman Personality Type Assessment
https://www.bravermantest.com/

I Feel - Emotional Word Wheel - The Feel Wheel - Australian English
https://feelingswheel.com/

King James Bible The Preserved and Living Word of God
https://www.kingjamesbibleonline.org/

An Encyclopedia Britannica Company
https://Merriam-webster.com

Poetry Foundation
https://www.poetryfoundation.org/poems/52702/the-bridge-builder

The Emperor's New Clothes
https://en.wikipedia.org/wiki/The_Emperor%27s_New_Clothes

https://Dictionary.com

https://www.etymonline.com

https://www.brainyquote.com

https://www.thelawofattraction.com/what-is-the-law-of-attraction/

https://wikidiff.com

https://www.successconsciousness.com/blog/law-of-attraction/law-of-attraction-definitions/

Notes:

"Stupid splashes."
Mindset Master Key #150

Notes:

"Knowledge comes from your successes,
 Wisdom comes from your failures."
Mindset Master Key #147

Notes:

"Keep it 100"
Unknown

www.ingramcontent.com/pod-product-compliance
Lightning Source LLC
Chambersburg PA
CBHW030557230426
43661CB00054B/2166